MODERN LETTER WRITING COURSE

An unparalleled & unprecedented 30-day course to writing simple, sharp and attractive letters

Writen by
Arun Sagar 'Anand'

Translated by
Editorial Board

Published by:

V&S PUBLISHERS
F-2/16, Ansari Road, Daryaganj, New Delhi-110002
☎ 011-23240026, 011-23240027 • *Fax:* 011-23240028
E-mail: info@vspublishers.com • *Website:* www.vspublishers.com

Branch : Hyderabad
5-1-707/1, Brij Bhawan (Beside Central Bank of India Lane)
Bank Street, Koti, Hyderabad - 500 095
☎ 040-24737290
E-mail: vspublishershyd@gmail.com

Follow us on:

For any assistance sms **VSPUB** to **56161**

All books available at **www.vspublishers.com**

© Copyright: V&S PUBLISHERS
ISBN 978-93-505702-0-3
Edition 2013

The Copyright of this book, as well as all matter contained herein (including illustrations) rests with the Publishers. No person shall copy the name of the book, its title design, matter and illustrations in any form and in any language, totally or partially or in any distorted form. Anybody doing so shall face legal action and will be responsible for damages.

Printed at : Param Offseters, Okhla, New Delhi-110020

Dedication

This book is dedicated to the young and dynamic Sri Sahil Gupta, Director of V& S Publishers who spared time off from his busy schedule to closely read the manuscript; and offered valuable suggestions to improve the quality of the book.

Publisher"s Note

It gives us pleasure to publish this book on letter writing named 'Modern Letter Writing Course". It had been our cherished desire to bring out a book on letter writing for readers in a systematic and scientific manner.

This book attempts to present rules for letter writing in all possible situations and circumstances. Despite the availability of e-mails, telephones, mobile phones, instant messaging etc, it is ultimately the correspondence made through letters that matters; whether it is an issue concerning personal, social, family or business ties. Letters have retained their preponderance in a milieu of communications the way books have remained strong among all readable materials – whether available in printed or digital forms.

Using words in simple and day-to-day language, this book tries to exemplify every kind of letters ordinarily people take recourse to while writing on personal, commercial, business or official subjects.

This book, **Modern Letter Writing Course** is presumed to be completed within 30 days. All that is needed by a diligent reader is to devote time to comprehend a few pages each single day and then practise its usage. Ample examples have been given to simplify the process of learning. A CD comes free with the book incorporating all letters given.

We sincerely hope the readers would make the best use of this book to master the art and science of letter writing in all situations and circumstances.

Preface

Innumerable means are available that facilitate communications between two individuals or businesses. New technologies are coming up every other day that expand the sphere of communicating one"s thoughts and ideas. Despite the ease with which telephones and e-mails have made their way into our lives, the uninterrupted run of letter writing continues to flourish. The art of writing has not lost its significance one bit; the way printed books continue with their monopoly in all reading materials. Radios and TVs are just but a small diversion.

It is difficult to fathom the importance of the letter and of its writing. The letter plays a second part only to conversation and to personal contact. Because of the letter no one remains a stranger, and to the letter writer no part of the civilized world is inaccessible. New forms of communication have come up but they all remain the same in essence – conveying an idea or two.

The letter connects persons, and is the vehicle of the progress of humankind. While neither the writer of this book, nor anyone else, can teach by printed page, or orally, the great science or art of letter writing, it is hoped that the contents of this book will be of at least indirect assistance to everyone who uses the mails, and 'every one" includes the whole world.

This book uses simple and everyday language to tell readers the correct way and polished manners to write personal, commercial, business and official letters on all occasions.

A number of model examples have been included to write skilfully individual, personal, family, social and business letters besides others forms of communications written for specific needs - jobs, banking, insurance, e-mails, etc. The examples are intended to help readers to learn the basics and master the science of perfect letter writing. Manner of writing official letters have been extensively given, such as, notification, oath, declaration, press communiqué, press note, ordinance, tender, auction, notice, government official letters, memo and sanction letters.

The book is to be used as a guide so that the reader develops a succinct way of writing high quality letters. I hope that by making the best use of this book not only the ones associated with writing official and other kinds of letters, even the private sector employees, housewives and other interested people would start writing impressive and attractive letters efficiently and easily.

I look forward to suggestions and criticisms for making the forthcoming edition of the book more useful.

– Arun Sagar 'Anand"

Contents

Section – 1 : Before Beginning to Write

1. Letter Writing 15
2. Letter Writing: An Art 17
3. Before Beginning to Write a Letter 18
4. Letter Writing and its Importance 23

Section – 2 : Different Parts of a Letter

5. Different Parts of a Letter & Its Description 26

   ❋ Personal and Family Letters ❋ Parts of Personal Letters ❋ Form of Personal and Family Letters ❋ Letter to a Friend ❋ Business Letters ❋ Request for a Copy of the Catalogue Sourabh Electricals ❋ Reply to the Above Letter Bajaj Electricals Pvt. Ltd

Section – 3 : Personal Letter Unofficial Letter

6. Invitation Letters 33

   ❋ Griha Pravesh ❋ Naming Ceremony ❋ Inauguration of a Hotel ❋ Invitation for Dinner ❋ Felicitation ❋ (Accepting the Invitation) ❋ Declining the Invitation ❋ Dinner Invitation ❋ (Accepting the Invitation) (Declining the Invitation) ❋ Invitation for Refreshment ❋ Declining the Invitation ❋ Declining the Invitation ❋ Declining the Invitation ❋ Invitation to Participate in a Cultural Programme

7. Letters of Sympathy 61

   ❋ A Letter of Sympathy ❋ On Losing a Football Match at School ❋ Being Unsuccessful at a Competitive Examination ❋ Letter from a Father to his Son who has Lost his Job ❋ Factory Destroyed in Fire ❋ On Losing an Election ❋ On Being Attacked ❋ Theft in the House ❋ On Losing an Election ❋ On the Death of a Close Relative

8. Congratulatory Letters 71

   ❋ Congratulatory Letter on the Publication of a Magazine ❋ Congratulating a Friend on Topping the B.A. Exams and Getting Honoured with Gold Medal ❋ Congratulating a Friend on Getting a Ph.D Degree ❋ Greeting on the Birthday of a Friend ❋ Congratulatory Letter on Winning an Election ❋ Congratulatory Letter on Being Appointed as a

Lecturer ❈ Congratulations on Winning a Lottery ❈ Congratulations on the Birth of a Baby Boy/Girl

9. Regret Letters 80
   ❈ Regretting Failure to Submit an Article for the Magazine ❈ Inability to Attend a Marriage Function ❈ Seeking Excuse for Not Reaching on the Demise of Friend"s Father ❈ Seeking Excuse for Not Reaching the Kavya Sammelan ❈ Letter to Father Seeking Excuse for Falling into Bad Company

10. Letter of Recommendation 83
    ❈ Introducing a Friend to a Publisher for Publishing his/her Manuscript ❈ Recommending a Known Person for a Job ❈ Recommending a Suitable Person for a Job

11. Letters Expressing Obligation 88
    ❈ Letter Expressing Obligation to an Individual ❈ Obligatory Letters ❈ Social Obligatory Letter

12. Letters of Obligation, Condolence, etc. 97
    ❈ A Thank You Letter for Donating Books for the Library ❈ Thanking a Person for Returning the Lost Papers ❈ Condolence Letter to a Friend on the Death of his Mother ❈ Condolence Letter to a Friend on the Death of his Father ❈ Condolence Letter to a Friend on the Death of his Father ❈ Condolence Message

13. Descriptive Letters 100
    ❈ Descriptive Letters ❈ Letter to a Younger Brother Suggesting Ways to Stay Healthy ❈ Writing a Letter to Chacha/Chachi Wanting to Spend Holidays with Them ❈ Letter from a Pre-marriage Lover to his Beloved ❈ Travel-Related Letter ❈ My Haridwar Trip ❈ Mixed Type of Letters ❈ Letter to Wife ❈ A Letter to Husband ❈ Letter from a Student to a Teacher

Section – 4 : Social and Public letters

14. Social Correspondence 108
    ❈ Social Correspondence ❈ Suggestion for Prevention of Divorce ❈ Suggestion to an Editor ❈ Social Invitation

15. Letters of Complaint 111
    ❈ [Personal] Non-delivery of Money Order ❈ Unbecoming Behaviour of the Bus Conductor ❈ Non-functional Telephone ❈ Irregularities in the Supply of Gas Cylinders ❈ Complaint to Railway Authorities ❈ Complaint Regarding Damaged Product ❈ [Public] Irregularities in Power Supply ❈ Complaint Against Inadequate Water Supply ❈ Lethargy of Bank Staff ❈ Irregularities at Post Office ❈ Complaint against Dirt, Filth and Garbage in the Colony ❈ Sale of Subsidised Kerosene Oil in the Market

16. Letters to the Editor 122

✿ Requesting the Editor to Publish an Article ✿ Annual Subscription ✿ News Regarding Fire ✿ Fire Engulfed 50 Houses in the Slum Colony ✿ Dead Body Found ✿ Unidentified Body Found ✿ Truck – Jeep Collision ✿ Truck – Jeep Collision: Two Dead, Four Injured ✿ A Suggestion Regarding Materials Published in Special Section of Newspapers ✿ To Check Smoking ✿ Request Not to Display Advertisements in the Middle of a Programme ✿ Misbehaviour of Driver/Conductor of a Bus ✿ On Gambling in the Colonies ✿ Bad Elements, Ruffians in the Society ✿ To Prevent Road Accidents ✿ Adulteration at the Petrol Pump ✿ Dirt, Garbage and Lack of Cleanliness in the Locality ✿ Opinion on Rising Prices ✿ Relentless Price Rise ✿ Opinion : Today"s Indian Woman is Empowered ✿ Today"s Indian Woman is Empowered ✿ [Appeal] ✿ Donation Sought for Treatment ✿ Donation for Treatment of Blood Cancer ✿ Appeal for a Kidney ✿ Appeal for Donating a Kidney

17. Correspondence with Insurance Companies 139

    ✿ Making Enquiry

18. Correspondence with Post Offices 140

    ✿ Regarding a VPP Sent ✿ Seeking a Post Box Number ✿ Change of Address to the Post Office ✿ Non-Delivery of Mails in Time ✿ Job-Related Letters

Section – 5 : Job-Related Letters

19. Job-Related Letters 144

    ✿ Application for the Post of Salesman ✿ Application for the Post of an Accountant ✿ Written Examination/Interview – Notification ✿ Anmol Vastra Bhandar ✿ Verification of Credentials of the Selected Candidates ✿ Enquiry Regarding Credentials ✿ Appointment Letter

Section – 6 : Business Letters

20. Business Letters 158

    ✿ Parts of a Business Letter Constituents of a Good Business Letter ✿ Types of Commercial Letters ✿ Regular Commercial Correspondence ✿ Confirmation of Receipt of a Letter ✿ Letters of Acknowledgement ✿ Letters of Confirmation

21. Letters Regarding Products 182

    ✿ Logistics Loading and Transportation ✿ Supplementary Letters ✿ Correspondence Regarding Agreement ✿ Demi-Official Letters ✿ Congratulatory Messages ✿ Letters of Sympathy ✿ Sales Letters

Section – 7 : Government Communications and Letters

22. Government Communications and Letters 213
23. Notification 216

✤ Government of India Ministry of Education ✤ Government of India Ministry of Finance, New Delhi ✤ State Bank of India New Delhi ✤ Government of India Ministry of External Offices, New Delhi ✤ Reserve Bank of India New Delhi ✤ Government of India Ministry of Agriculture ✤ Oath ✤ Government of Madhya Pradesh Ministry of Public Administration ✤ Declaration ✤ Press Communiqué Office of the Executive Engineer Electricity Department (West Zone, Indore) ✤ Office of the Commissioners Municipal Corporation, Bhopal ✤ Madhya Pradesh Administration Ministry of Transport, Bhopal ✤ Commissioner Delhi Development Authority, New Delhi ✤ Government of India Ministry of Home Affairs ✤ Government of Uttar Pradesh Ministry of Sports and Youth Affairs, Lucknow ✤ Press Note Government of Tamil Nadu ✤ Department of Home Affairs, Chennai ✤ Education Loan ✤ Ordinance Government of India Ministry of Law, New Delhi ✤ Correction and Corrigendum Government of Madhya Pradesh ✤ Department Corrigendum Education ✤ Auction Notice ✤ Awards for Information Regarding Prisoners Escaped from Jail ✤ No Action against Striking Employees ✤ Education Department, Indore ✤ Government of India Department of Administrative Affairs ✤ Department Linguistics ✤ Government of Maharashtra (Minister of Name of the Department)

Section – 8 : Receipt and Dispatch of Letters

24. Receipt & Dispatch Department and its Importance..254
25. Office...258
26. Influence of Correspondence 260

Section – 9 : Bank and E-mail Letters

27. Bank-related Correspondence...262
    ✤ Refusal by a Bank to Honour a Cheque Punjab National Bank ✤ Stop Payment Instruction ✤ Letter to a Party Complaining about Bouncing of its Cheque ✤ Application for Housing Loan ✤ Requesting Bank to Pay Telephone Bills from Account
28. E-mails 268

Section – 1
Before Beginning to Write

Letter Writing

Letter writing has become an important component in social life. The world appears to be interconnected by one way or another. No one has the time to meet another person as much as one would wish.

Letter writing is as old as humanity. Pigeons were used to carry messages in early times. There existed no postal facility then. Things moved on but what didn"t change course was the means of letter writing.

A person can continue to be in touch with another person, wherever he may be, by means of letters. Psychological studies reveal that:

❑ A person wants to preserve whatever he things or visualizes. He wants to share this with someone close. This he can do by means of communicating through letter writing.

❑ People who have spent years in jail reveal that but for maintaining touch with friends and relatives by letter writing, their thought processes, which is alive and kicking, would have dried up long ago.

❑ Pandit Jawaharlal Nehru"s letters to his daughter Indira Gandhi has become historical in true sense. Its relevance is for the posterity. That"s one reason why letters of great people are compiled for the benefit of the coming generations. Letters written by Lenin, Churchill, Mussolini, Napoleon, Hitler and Abraham Lincoln have made them immortal.

❑ Letter writing protects one from excitement, emotions, anger, etc. It is said that Abraham Lincoln used to start writing letters whenever angry. He would download his anger using the means of letter writing. Such letters he would always, instead of sending to the intended recipient, read and reread later to analyse what made him angry in the first place.

❑ If a person talks about his pain, ordinarily others wouldn"t pay much attention. Instead, they would act out the 'sympathy" part. No real feelings. But when the same pain is put down in writing, others try to understand the underlying idea behind the anguish and work out ways to help out.

❑ Letters strengthen the bonds among people. Pen-friendship is a testimony to this fact. People across the world can learn about one another. This helps strengthen cultural and social ties.

Letter writing is a reflection of times. A letter written today may have words like mobile phone, computer, television, google, facebook, internet, etc. We can, similarly, know about the history or geography of one country or another. Dress habits, culture, etc. get mirrored through letters.

Mentioned below are a few points we must take into consideration while writing:
- Nothing should be written that may compromise the social harmony.
- Letters must keep one another"s interest in mind.
- Letters should focus primarily on human welfare and not politics.
- Nothing irrelevant should find space in a letter.
- The language used should be easy and simple.
- A letter should reflect honesty; not hypocrisy.
- A letter should be brief and to the point.

Letter Writing: An Art

Letter writing has a bearing on our personal and social life. They reflect the way we conduct ourselves in society. To know a person, reading a few letters written by him is enough. Letters would reveal the working and thought process of his mind at different times in different situations. The letters symbolise the psychology, emotions, sense of belongings, personal relations and social equations, a person maintains.

A person has become a combination of various pulls and pressures. This finds expression though correspondence. Without letters or other modes of communications, it is difficult to maintain equilibrium in friendship, relations, social mores, work culture, business, polity, etc. The success and failure in life also depends a great deal upon our methods of correspondence. The more successful one is in letter writing, the more successful he is likely to become in future.

The habit of letter writing starts developing right from the student life. Such letters are written to parents, teachers and friends. These reflect the bonds of emotional attachment.

As soon as one enters the adult life, the letters acquire the edge of love, feelings and attachment.

Where personal relations are concerned, letters mostly portray closeness and empathy.

If you want to become a prolific letter writer, please pay attention to the following:

- Letter should be logical, short, crisp and clear.
- The presentation should be scientific, not full of emotions. Official and managerial letters should be built around solid matters, straightforward and to the point.
- The letter should be developed around proper reference and context. It must be clear, else confusion may arise. Before dispatching a letter, one should read it as if the receiver is reading it. Check everything is clear and accurate. If not, make changes where necessary.
- Never write a letter when angry.
- Always take care of your goodwill.
- A letter should be balanced, short and precise.

Before Beginning to Write a Letter

A letter is an image of the writer, his attitude, his personality. A letter is talk upon paper; but it is not as easy to write as it is to tell your story in spoken words, because when you talk, your audience is before you, and you can better adapt your words to the receiver who is present, than to one who is absent. If what you say when you talk is not right, and does not have the desired effect, you are likely to have opportunity to explain. What you say in a letter, however, must stand as it is, and is not subject to immediate correction, change or even a 'retake" much like we have in films. Therefore, the letter must be prepared with more care, and with more attention to detail, than is necessary for the spoken word.

It has been said, and with much truth, that nobody can write a letter, or any document, which is guaranteed to be fully and correctly understood by its receiver. The letter writer, therefore, must do his best, for the more care he gives to his letter, the greater likelihood there is of its being properly interpreted by its receiver.

Perfection is impossible, but there is a vast difference between a carelessly thrown-together letter and one which is intelligently written. A large part of the business of the world is conducted by correspondence; and no one can maintain his position without the writing of social letters.

While this book attempts to present rules for letter writing, it must be admitted that outside of the fundamental principles, it is difficult to instruct any one so that he may become, by these instructions alone, a prolific letter writer. Individual judgement and common sense play important parts upon the stage of letter writing. One may be helped by suggestions, and even by rules; but instruction alone is not sufficient. He must put himself into his letters. Proficiency exists only when one realizes their importance, and lets each experience aid him in producing better results. The book doesn"t aim to present more than a few forms of the body of a letter, because such arbitrary examples would be of little use to any proficient letter writer; and the indifferent one, using them, would make his letters framed and confined. One should, then, become familiar with suitable forms, and should adapt them to his conditions, but should not copy verbatim the style or wording of this book or any other for that matter.

A letter writer must keep the following in mind:

Clarity

A letter writer should be clear about the subject matter of the letter. It should be in plain and simple language so that the reader immediately gets to the bottom of the content. Confusion should be avoided at all costs.

Fullness/Absoluteness

Not only a letter should be clear in explaining things, but it should be complete as well. Nothing should be written that is out of context, nor any topic should be repeated. If something comes to mind after the letter has been written, then P.S.(Post Script) written below the letter serves the purpose. The subject missed out of the main letter is mentioned in P.S.

Ease

Simplicity is the lifeblood of any letter. It must be written with ease and appear logical moving from one idea to another. Difficult words have to be avoided. Small and short sentences make a letter easy to understand.

In Short

Brevity is the soul of a letter. It should also be complete in all respects without missing out on anything relevant. Unnecessary verbosity mars the ease in understanding the text matter.

Effective

Words must be used with care and caution. Only popular words and in current usage convey the meaning to an average reader. Letter should be interesting so that the recipient finds it interesting to read.

Manners

Language used should be polite and full of respect and etiquette. Courtesy breeds courtesy. Correct salutations make for a prompt reply. This fact must not be overlooked under any circumstances.

Attractive

Appearance of a letter enhances its attraction, makes it more readable, and subconsciously forces the reader to take note of the contents. The language of the letter deserves careful attention. Name and address should be written with accurately. No one likes to see his name misspelt.

Paper

A good quality paper draws the attention of the reader and makes for a good impression. Whereas students tend to use colourful and fancy papers, the grown-ups go for good quality plain papers. Ordinary papers are good enough for day-to-day mails; light-weight papers should be preferred for air mails. This reduces the expenses on postage.

Pen & Ink

Coloured inks, other than blue or black, should be used only during special occasions. Coloured inks don"t find approval from most people.

Writing with a pencil is a big No, while writing a letter. They become difficult to read or make out. *Therefore, every letter should be written with a pen.*

Accuracy & Cleanliness

Every sentence must be complete and carry a definite meaning. It should be easy to read and understand. While writing a business letter, special care must be taken regarding a bill, *hundi*, book of accounts, other commercial details, failing which the goodwill of the firm may be compromised.

Satisfactory

The credibility of a business letter hinges on the clarity and completeness with regard to details. Confusion at all costs should be avoided. The letter must clearly mention the weight, price, type, quality, amount and discount regarding the product. Making a mention of the available guarantee increases the value of the product and enhances the image of the firm.

Systematic

Points raised in the letter should follow an established sequence. Only one issue should be mentioned under a single point. Long sentences must be avoided. The letter, if necessary, should be made attractive by going in for an additional paragraph.

At Proper Time

Delay hurts a business and its growth. It hits the image of the firm as well. Letters should be promptly replied. If it is not possible to reply with sought-after information, an acknowledgement of the letter must be sent. Make a point to apologise, if for any reason, reply couldn"t be made in time.

Planning

A letter should be properly planned before writing. *Clarity is of utmost importance.* The reader must comprehend the subject matter of the letter. Respectful and polite words make the reader favourably inclined towards the writer.

Writing

A letter reflects the personality of the writer. Hence, it is important for a writer to be careful in the choice of words or sentences.

A letter may give out the establishment and line of organization, a writer has in his work ethics. *Good style and polished manners leave a sound impression on the recipient.*

Envelope

An envelope should be carefully chosen, capable of reflecting the image of the sender. The name of the recipient should begin close to the centre of the envelope and about one inch below the top edge. It should be followed by C/O (where required). This should be followed by House No, Lane, Locality, Name of the town/city, PIN Code, etc.

We can write Mr/Mrs/Sri/Smt, etc. before the name of a gentleman/lady. 'Esq" is often written before the name of any distinguished person. For an unmarried girl, the term, 'Miss" is used. Whereas 'To" is written in English, the term, 'Sewa Men" is used in Hindi.

Beginning to Write a Letter

While writing a letter, the writer should mention his 'address" on the top right hand side of the paper. This is followed by the 'date" right below the address. If the address is already printed on the paper, there is no need to write the address afresh. The name and address of the recipient is written on the left side of the paper. The form of writing is mainly used in business correspondence. It facilitates the office clerk to enter the sender"s and recipient"s address in the dispatch register. However, in personal letters, the address of the recipient is not written.

Subject of the Letter

There is little point elaborating at this stage on the subject matter of a letter. This is fully explained in subsequent chapters. It is enough to understand that it is the 'subject" that necessitates writing of any letter. The subject is the reason for entering into any correspondence. We have compiled a series of letters in the following pages taking note of various circumstances that directly or indirectly suggest us to write a letter. The readers would be able to understand the manner and presentation of writing letters in the most appropriate and modern style.

Correct Style of Writing

The writer must choose words with care. A word wrongly used could change the meaning of the letter altogether. The meaning of the letter may become confusing or even irrelevant. The words that convey the intended meaning should only be used.

Similarly, the writer should pay attention to the *accuracy of the words also.* Correct spellings of the words are important. Unlike spoken words, there is no chance to recall the word that has been put down. The letter will stay as it is, wrong words, unintended words or confusing words. You can"t wish them away. Therefore, be careful while using any word.

Use of Comma

Sometimes placing a 'comma" at a wrong place can change the meaning of the sentence. You wanted to convey one thing but by placing the 'comma" at a wrong place, the idea gets changed. In fact, even the opposite meaning could also be conjured up. The writer must put a full stop after completion of a sentence. An explanatory sign is marked as ('!"). While quoting someone else"s sentence, inverted comma ('..."') is indicated. Mark of interrogation ('?") is used whenever the sentence asks for an answer.

Typing Letters

Some opine that personal letters shouldn"t be typed. Intimacy is lost and formality is introduced. But many people have started sending personal letters duly typed. The advantage typed letters introduce is ease in reading and simplicity in capturing the theme.

Business Letters

The major difference between success and failure of a business is attributed to the way correspondence is done. *Writing business letters is a great art.* It is considered important to make correspondence in a timely manner; and without delay. Business letters are divided into following five sections:

1. Sales-related correspondence
2. Day-to-day regular correspondence
3. Accounts-related correspondence
4. Advertisement-related correspondence
5. Establishment-related correspondence

The above mentioned letters can be sub-divided into many other sections. Irrespective of sections or sub-sections, every correspondence ultimately ends up contributing to sales. No letter should be delayed in responding quickly, more so a business one. *A prompt reply boosts a firm"s image.* Moreover, it is a matter of courtesy and business ethics.

Business letters should preferably be typed. Many large organisations make use of a shorthand writer to dictate letters for eventual typing.

Closing a Letter

Whereas in English language, letters written in the first person close with the words, 'Yours Truly" or 'Yours faithfully", the corresponding Hindi words are 'Aapka" or 'Tumhara". 'Aapka" is used only as a mark of respect for an elder person. Form of closing a letter requires more care and attention in business letters than in personal ones.

Business Signature

Business letters should be signed such that the recipient finds practically no difficulty in deciphering his name. If the writing is illegible, his name should be clearly typed below the signature.

Goodwill of the Firm

An attractive manner of letter writing impresses the recipient and enhances the goodwill of the firm. Care must be taken to see that the image of the firm gets a leg-up with every correspondence.

Letter Writing and its Importance

Letter writing is a process of exchanging communications by means of letters. It could be between two firms, organisations, customers, or personal relations. It could be between a firm and a customer. In fact, any exchange of ideas between two individuals or entities is broadly classified as *correspondence through letters*.

Importance of Letter Writing

Letters are an important form of communication. It is a medium to exchange views. Following points constitute the major components of letter writing:

- **Written medium of expression** – Letter is a medium of exchange of ideas between two letter writers. It can be resorted to when inconvenience is experienced while making any oral communication.

- **Simplicity in record keeping** – It is difficult to keep a record of oral discussions. But a written communication can be conveniently filed for future reference. It can be gone through as and when required.

- **Opportune time to use considered thoughts** – It sometimes happens that we speak something that we never intended to say. But a letter writer saves himself from such undesirable situations. If a word has been erroneously written, it can always be amended, modified and reset for improved impression.

- **Continuity in relationship** – Letters help in cementing the relationship between two persons or firms even if they are not meeting each other on a regular basis.

- **As a representative** – *A letter in essence is a representative of the writer.* While a personal letter represents an individual, a business letter does the same for an organisation.

- **As a medium of complaint** – *A complaint made orally is not as effective as a written one.* A written one stands testimony to the proof that some difficulty or inconvenience is experienced against which redressal has been sought. It forms part of a complaint register.

- **Conveyor of pleasure and pain** – A letter is a communication that can convey good news or an inconvenient one. It acts as a postman who can bring in news of all sorts – good, bad or ugly.

- **Government"s messages** – The government circulates its orders, information, news, etc. through the medium of letters.

- **Proof** – The letters stand proof of a document circulated or conveyed.
- **As a literature** – Writers write books, notes, novels, poems, etc. and place before the general public for recreation, or information or enjoyment. This eliminates the sense of loneliness.
- **As a social reformer** – Various newspapers and magazines earmark space for people to write their views, comments or complaints against the ills existing in the society. The columns represent both, the bouquets and the brickbats.
- **As a critic** – Letters are means of critical appreciation written by a reader of any literary work or happening of common public importance.
- **Economic medium** – In these days of busy life, letters are a very economical medium to remain in touch with family, friends and relatives. They are equally useful in maintaining business relationships.

Section – 2
Different Parts of a Letter

Different Parts of a Letter & Its Description

Letter writing is an art to communicate an idea to another person in a simple and straightforward manner. It should be brief, to-the-point and devoid of difficult words.

It is impossible to visualise the importance of writing a letter. A letter connects two persons staying miles away. It is also the vehicle of business establishments.The letter ranks next only to conversation and to personal contact. Because of letters even strangers get to know one another, and to the letter writer, no civilised world remains inaccessible.

In these days of mobile phones, e-mails, videos and text messages, letter writing may seem totally outdated. But it"s truly an art that will always remain in reckoning. A letter brings back nostalgic feelings, fond remembrances that modern technology cannot produce. Facebook may be great for circulating what one is doing in the evening, and e-mail is superb for quick exchanges on important ideas. But when it comes to sharing one"s sincere thoughts, true sympathies, ardent love, and deep gratitude, words moving along invisible superhighways will never suffice. You need a handwritten note.

While writing any letter, it is important to keep in mind the context and components of the subject matter.

Personal and Family Letters

Letters that family members write to one another to know the welfare are called Personal Letters. It is the most common type, and also the most prevalent. These are written between friends, family members or any two people with close ties. *It uses a more informal tone.* It can be written just to say, 'Hello", or express personal matters.

Parts of Personal Letters

(1) Address of the writer
(2) Date
(3) Salutation
(4) Subject
(5) Subject matter
(6) Signature
(7) Name and address of the addressee

(Sample-1)
Form of Personal and Family Letters

(1) Address of the writer
(2) Date
(3) Salutation
(4) Subject
(5) Subject matter
(6) Signature
(7) Name and address of the addressee

(Sample-2)

```
       ................
       Salutation
       Subject matter _____
       _____
       _____


   Date..............                              Signature
                                                   Address
```

(Sample-1)
Letter to a Friend

1809, Subhash Mohalla
Gandhi Nagar, Delhi – 110031
Dated:

Dear Ved,

    You cleared the B.Com examination in first division, whereas I could not. I had hoped to clear the exam if not securing a second division. I am at a loss of words how and what to write to you.

    This year, I was afflicted more with the idea of becoming a class representative and in becoming a student leader. This led me to come into contact with students who are less serious in classes; as well as involved into frivolous activities. The outcome is there for you to see - a disastrous result. I have, forthwith, decided to abandon this slush outright, join the group of good students and be dedicated and sincere towards studies.

    Please convey my regards to your parents.

    Waiting for your reply!

Yours own,
Manoj

Sri Ved Kumar
65/2, Joshi Bhavan
Loha Khan, Police Lines
Ajmer, Rajasthan

Business Letters

A business letter is short, straightforward and addressed in a polite manner. It is written by one business firm to another. Every business house desires to establish and retain good commercial relationship with other firms. This is mainly done through effective business correspondence. Ordinarily, business letters are written to elicit enquiry, order placement, sending a sample, agency/franchisee request, or any other commercial matter. Despite modern communication and technology coming into play, interaction by correspondence continues to be the final word.

Business communication should be precise, polite and to-the-point. There is no place for verbosity. It should be limited to one single spaced page, if possible. When you write a business letter, you must presume that your audience is busy and has limited time. Always remember your audience wants to know the 'bottom line".

There are times when a 'note" is appended on the bottom left side of the letter, below the signature when some important matter has come to mind that must be communicated. Some businesses use this method to highlight an important matter to which they want the attention of the recipient to be drawn into.

Following are the parts of business letters :
(1) Name and address of the sender
(2) Date
(3) Letter Number
(4) Name and address of the recipient
(5) Salutation
(6) Subject matter
(7) Action sought
(8) Signature and name
(9) Designation
10) Enclosure:
(11) Note (P.S.) Post Script:

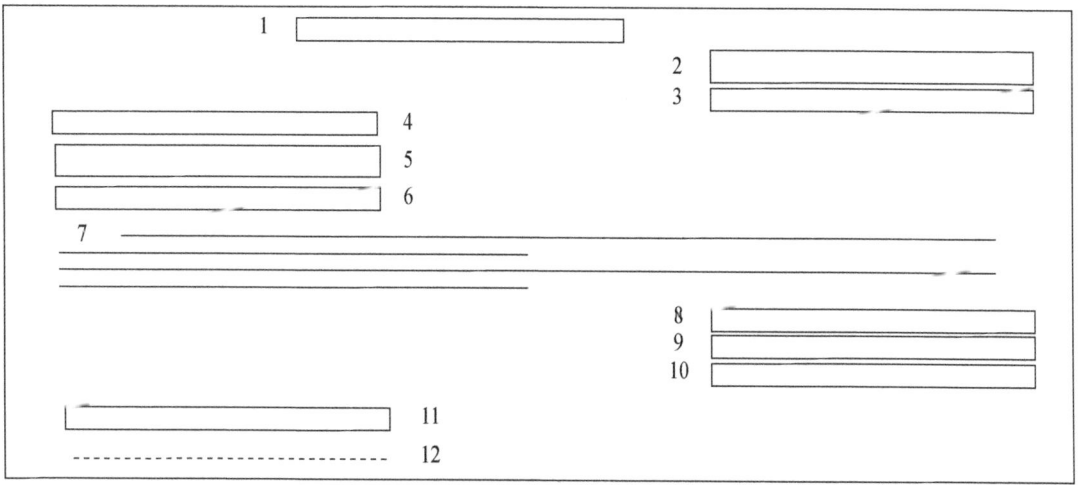

Different Parts of a Letter & Its Description

(Sample-1)
Request for a Copy of the Catalogue
Sourabh Electricals

G-9, White House
Ring Road, Paschim Vihar
New Delhi –110063
Date: 20/11/XX

Telephone:
Mobile:
Letter No – 10/08/XX

To,
    Messrs. Bajaj Electricals Pvt.Ltd
    Deen Dayal Road
    Mumbai – 400006

Dear Sir,

    We are a wholesaler of household electrical goods. In view of the onset of summer season, we would like to stock fans, coolers and exhaust fans to meet the demand.

    We request you to send us your latest price list on the above mentioned items along with your most competitive commercial terms.

Yours faithfully,
For Saurabh Electricals
Saurabh Sharma
Manager

(Sample-2)
Reply to the Above Letter
Bajaj Electricals Pvt. Ltd

18 B, Deen Dayal Road
Mumbai – 400006
Date: 25/11/XX

To

    M/S Saurabh Electricals
    G-9, White House
    Ring Road, Paschim Vihar
    New Delhi – 110063

Dear Sir,

    Thank you for your letter that we received last evening. As desired, we are sending you our latest price list for your consideration. We are sure, you would find the rates of fans, coolers and exhaust fans manufactured by us much lower in price than that of others. Because of better quality and economical pricing, these products are in strong demand in the market place. As a matter of policy, we offer a discount of 20% only to such wholesale dealers who place orders not below ₹ 10,000/-. The responsibility to dispatch correct supply rests with us.

Yours faithfully,
Development Officer
For Sales Manager
Encl: Price List

Different Parts of a Letter & Its Description

Section – 3
Personal Letter
Unofficial Letter

Invitation Letters

There are many occasions when a person wishes to invite others to celebrate some memorable moments. Inauguration, marriage, *griha pravesh*, birthday, etc., are some of those occasions.

If the occasion demands compassion or condolence, a letter to such effect can convey the feeling adequately. Sometimes, we commit some blunder, though unintentionally, and come to realise later. In such situations, it is quite appropriate to seek forgiveness. At times, we can"t make it to the place, despite our wanting to do so. This also demands, suitable letter of apology. We should also thank a person for any help he may have extended to us. Courtesy demands that we should correspond through letters on occasions, such as,

- ❊ Invitation, ❊ Sympathy, ❊ Congratulations, ❊ Regret Letters,
- ❊ Recommendations, ❊ Obligations, ❊ Condolence, etc.

(Sample-1)
Griha Pravesh

Dear Deveshji

You would be pleased to know that the 'Griha Pravesh" ceremony of our new house will take place at 10.00 in the morning on Moday dated...

You are cordially invited, along with all the family members to grace this occasion. We hope, you will oblige us with your presence.

Yours truly,
Sanjay Suri
22, Milansar Apartment
Near Piragarhi, Paschim Vihar
New Delhi - 110063

(Sample-2)
Naming Ceremony

Dear Nareshji,

You would be pleased to know that we have been blessed with the birth of a son recently. To celebrate the occasion, a 'Namkaran function" has been fixed to take place on Friday, dated…at 5.00 in the evening.

Please accept our humble invitation to grace the ceremony and bless the newborn child along with all your family members.

Yours truly,
Avinash Khatri
21, Milansar Apartment
Near Piragarhi, Paschim Vihar
New Delhi - 110063

(Sample-3)
Inauguration of a Hotel

To

Sri/Smt…

Warm greetings!

You would be pleased to know that on the occasion of launching our new hotel 'Samrat", a 'Satyanarayan Puja" has been organised at 11.00 in the morning on Sunday, dated…

On this auspicious occasion, may we request you to kindly visit us along with your family members and close friends, accept the 'prasad" and help us relish the sense of fulfilment.

Yours truly,
Anand Singh

R.S.V.P.
Samrat Hotel
Address:

(Sample-4)
Invitation for Dinner

Dear Sunil Sagarji,

Warm greetings!

You would be pleased to know that my son, Manish has been selected in the IAS.

To celebrate the occasion, we are hosting a dinner at our house at 9.00 in the evening on Sunday, dated…

We hope you would oblige us with your honourable presence.

Yours truly,
Arvind Anand
Address:

(Sample-5)
Felicitation

A warm invitation is extended to
Smt and Sri…
to attend a dinner party hosted on 21 April XX
to honour and felicitate
Smt and Sri Vijay Kumar I.G.
We hope you will kindly honour the invitation.

Yours sincerely,
Devendra Sharma
Address:

Time: 5.00 p.m.
Dress: Formal
R.S.V.P.

(Sample-6)
Felicitation

A warm invitation is extended to
Smt and Sri...
to attend a dinner party hosted at Hotel Janpath on
21/4/XX at 5.00 p.m.
to honour and felicitate
Smt and Sri Vijay Kumar I.G.
We hope you will kindly honour the invitation,
and grace the occasion.

Yours sincerely,
Devendra Sharma
Address:

Hotel Janpath
R.S.V.P.

(Sample-7)
Felicitation

Devendra Sharma cordially invites Smt/Sri... to a dinner function hosted at Hotel Janpath on 21/4/20XX at 5.00 p.m. in the honour of Smt/Sri Vijay Kumar, Inspector General.

I hope you will kindly grace the occasion.

Address
R.S.V.P.

(Sample-8)
(Accepting the Invitation)

Dear Devendra Sharmaji,

It feels nice to receive your invitation card. We will surely attend the function hosted at Hotel Janpath on 21/4/20XX at 5.00 p.m. in the honour of Smt/Sri Vijay Kumar. Being invited to such an august function is a testimony to your dedication and sincerity.

Your friend,
Bhuvanesh Ranjan
Address

Dated…

(Sample-9)
Declining the Invitation

Dear Devendra Sharmaji,

We are truly grateful to you for the courtesy extended to us to join the dinner function hosted in the honour of Smt/Sri Vijay Kumarji, I.G. We regret to inform you that due to ill health of my mother, it will not be possible for us to join you. I hope you will appreciate my inconvenience.

Your friend,
Bhuvanesh Ranjan
Address

Dated…

(Sample-10)
Dinner Invitation

Chaitanya 'Suman" extends an invitation to Smt/Sri…
to attend a dinner being hosted at Hotel Samrath (address)
on 4/3/20XX at 5.00 p.m.
Trust the couple would grace the occasion.

Dated…
Address
R.S.V.P.

(Sample-11)

Smt/Sri…is requested to attend
a dinner being hosted at Hotel Samrath
on 4/3/20XX at 5.00 p.m.

Hotel Samrath
Address
Dated…
R.S.V.P.

(Sample-12)
(Accepting the Invitation)

Dear Sumanji,

Thank you for your kind invitation. Your Bhabhi felt happy when I handed her the invitation. We look forward to partake the dinner at 5.00 p.m. on 4/3/XX.

Yours,
Aman Srivastava
Address

Dated…

(Sample-13)
(Declining the Invitation)

Dear Chaitanyaji,

Thank you for your kind invitation. I really wished to sit with you and relish the dinner. Unfortunately, on 4/3/20XX, I have to go out of town on an urgent work. I hope you will appreciate my inconvenience and would excuse my absence.

Yours,
Aman Srivastava
Address

Dated…

Invitation for Refreshment

Invitation for refreshment is sent in a manner identical to 'dinner". Replies to such invitation are sent on similar lines except that 'refreshment" is written in place of 'dinner".

In India, the concept of lunch, dinner and breakfast is quite different from the one seen in western countries.

It is important to convey acceptance or otherwise of every invitation in a timely manner so as to keep the host informed suitably.

(Sample-1)

Declining the Invitation

Dear friend,

Thank you for your kind invitation. I really wished to sit with you and relish the dinner. Unfortunately, I will not be able to take part because I have already accepted an invitation elsewhere on this particular day. I hope you will appreciate my inconvenience and would excuse my absence.

Yours sincerely,
Ravi Saxena
Address

Dated...

(Sample-2)
Declining the Invitation

Dear friend,

Your obedient pupil warmly thanks you for your kind invitation for dinner. I regret with heavy heart, to inform you that it will not be possible for me to attend the dinner due to the illness of my wife. I hope you will appreciate my inconvenience and would excuse my absence.

Yours pupil,
Vidya Sagar
Address

Dated…

(Sample-3)
Declining the Invitation

Dear Damini,

Thank you for your kind invitation for dinner. It is a matter of utmost satisfaction to receive one. I imagine, it would have been wonderful to sit with you and enjoy the dinner. I regret to inform you that due to the sickness of my son, I will have to attend to him since there is none to take care. I hope you will appreciate my inconvenience and would excuse my absence.

Your younger brother,
Anant Upadhyay
Address

Dated…

(Sample-4)
Invitation to Participate in a Cultural Programme

Dear Brajeshji,

I have invited a few of my close friends in the evening of the 25th April, 20XX for dinner. On that day itself, India-fame Yatin Sahani would be performing his new play in the local auditorium. It is my sincere desire that you should spare time to grace the occasion and allow the gathering present therein to enjoy your wit, light jokes and humour. My friends have been pressurising me for quite some time the need for your presence. I hope you will be kind enough to honour the request of my friends.

Yours sincerely,
Jayesh Saxena

Dated...
R.S.V.P.

(Sample-5)
Acceptance of the Invitation

Dear Jayeshji,

I am grateful for the invitation you have sent to witness the play being performed by India-fame Yatin Sahani in the local auditorium. Likewise, I am truly obliged to be invited to partake the dinner organised, just prior to the start of the play. I hope to enjoy an eventful evening.

Yours sincerely,
Brajesh

Dated...

(Sample-6)
Declining the Invitation

Dear friend,

    I am grateful to you for sending us an invitation to join a tea party followed by witnessing a football match. It is difficult to decline either of the events. Despite this, you can"t always turn away from social obligations. You might be remembering the old lady who stays on the upper floor of my house. She is not keeping well and is critical. Her condition necessitated me to take a day off yesterday. I hope you would appreciate my responsibility and would excuse me for declining the invitation.

Your sincerely,
Anuj Tripathi
Address

Dated…

(Sample-7)
Invitation to a Picnic

Dear Rajni,

    We have planned a picnic trip to Surajkund, the coming Sunday. We will be having our lunch there itself. It would be great to have you join us on this occasion. I hope you will accept our invitation.

Your brother,
Narottam Sehgal
Address

Dated…
R.S.V.P.

(Sample-8)
Acceptance of the Invitation

Dear Narottam,

    It is a pleasure to receive your invitation to the planned picnic trip to Surajkund, the coming Sunday. It"s enjoyable to go out with Bhabhi and Mataji. I would definitely join you on this occasion. In fact, I would be reaching your place by Saturday evening itself.

    Convey my regards to Mataji.

Yours affectionately,
Rajni
Address

Dated…

(Sample-9)
Declining the Invitation

Dear Narottam,

It is a pleasure to receive your invitation for a picnic trip to Surajkund, the coming Sunday. But I regret I will not be able to join you all. Your Jijaji is coming this Sunday along with a few of his friends. I am expected to take care of their convenience. Kindly convey my inability to Mataji to join you all to the picnic.

Yours affectionately,
Rajni
Address

Dated…

(Sample-10)

Invitation to a Show

Dear Dipti,

 Popular artist and dancer Sri Surajmal Maharaj is displaying his theatrics at the Kamani Auditorium tomorrow evening. I have already booked two seats. I would like you to join me in enjoying the show. I hope you will reach my house in time.

Yours truly,
Sagar
Address

Dated...
R.S.V.P.

(Sample-11)

Acceptance of the Invitation

Dear Sagar,

 It is great to know that world renowned artist and dancer Sri Surajmal Maharaj is displaying his theatrics at the Kamani Auditorium tomorrow evening. Your invitation came as a pleasant surprise to me. I would like to join you in enjoying the show. Be sure, I will reach your house in time.

Yours truly,
Dipti

Address
Dated...

Invitation Letters

(Sample-12)
Invitation Declined

Dear Sagar,

Thanks for your invitation. It is great to know that world renowned artist and dancer Sri Surajmal Maharaj is displaying his theatrics at the Kamani Auditorium tomorrow evening. I feel extremely sorry to decline your invitation to join you to witness the great dancer in action.

It so happened that my younger brother Bobby slipped from the roof and injured himself badly. We are afraid to move out not knowing when we would be needed. I hope you will excuse me for not joining yo.

Yours truly,
Dipti
Address

Dated...

(Sample-13)
Invitation to a Book Fair

Dear Anushka,

You would be pleased to know that a 7-day Book Fair is being organised at the Pragati Maidan in Delhi. Book publishers from India and abroad would be taking part in this event. I have decided to go to Delhi to visit this book fair. For quite some time, we have not met. I look forward to meeting you during this trip to Delhi.

Yours truly,
Nibhrant
Address

Dated...
R.S.V.P.

(Sample-14)
Acceptance of the Invitation

Dear Nibhrant,

    Thank you for your kind invitation to join you to visit the book fair being organised at the Pragati Maidan in Delhi. I have heard a lot about this great event. I too have not been able to meet you for long due to a hectic work schedule. I look forward to visiting the book fair with you in company.

Yours sincerely,
Anushka
Address

Dated…

(Sample-15)
Invitation Declined

Dear Nibhrant,

    Thank you for your kind invitation to join you to visit the book fair being organised at the Pragati Maidan in Delhi. I have heard a lot about this great event. But due to the increased workload in the office, I am not able to go home before 8 – 9 in the evening. I hope, next week, I may be able to take a few days break. Under the situation I am in presently, I would like to be excused from visiting the book fair.

Yours sincerely,
Anushka
Address

Dated…

Invitation Letters

(Sample-16)
Engagement Ceremony

Smt/Sri ...

Is requested to join the tea party organised on 3/3/20XX at 5.00 in the evening at the Shyam Banquet. A small function has been organised to celebrate the auspicious settlement of marriage of Ramesh with Kamlesh Kumari, M.A., daughter of Smt. and Sri Radhika Ramanji of Varanasi. Kindly grace the occasion along with your family members and honour us by your presence.

Humbly Solicited by,
Vijay Sabbarwal

Dated:
R.S.V.P.

(Sample-17)
Acceptance of the Invitation

Dear Sir,

We learnt with pleasure the auspicious settlement of marriage of Ramesh with Kamlesh Kumari, M.A., daughter of Smt. and Sri Radhika Ramanji of Varanasi. We would attend the tea party organised on this occasion.

Yours truly,
Naresh Pathak
Address

Dated:
R.S.V.P.

(Sample-18)
Declining the Invitation

Dear Sir,

 Warm greetings! We received your kind invitation and learnt with much delight the auspicious settlement of marriage of your son Ramesh with Kamlesh Kumari, M.A., daughter of Smt. and Sri Radhika Ramanji of Varanasi. Despite our strong desire to join you on this occasion, I am very sad to inform you that I am going to Chandigarh on an urgent assignment. I hope you will excuse my absence.

Yours
Naresh Pathak
Address

Dated:
R.S.V.P.

(Sample-19)
Marriage Invitation Card

!!Shubh Vivah!!
!! Sri Ganeshaya Namah!!
Aniket Singh
S/O Late Surendra Singh
Weds
Sunita Singh
D/O Late Jainendra Singh
On the auspicious and solemn occasion of two souls getting united, kindly bestow on the young couple your choicest blessings and honour us with your gracious presence.

Invitation Letters

Solicited by :   Requested by
Singh Family   Jai Narayan Singh
                                                                                                               Schedule

Dwarchar: Friday, 29th November, 7.00 Evening
Vivah: Friday, 29th November, 10.00 Evening
Vidai: Saturday, 30th November, 10.00 Morning

!!Venue!!
Navrang Hotel Cantt, Varanasi (UP)

Note: The *barat* party will depart from our village, Niamatganj on Friday, 29th November, 2011 at 12.00 noon by bus and reach Vishal Hotel, Cantt, Varanasi in the evening.

(Sample-20)

I feel honoured to inform Smt/Sri …that by the grace of God, the marriage of my son Suresh Khatri with Kavya Kumari, (D/O Smt/Sri Hari Nath Khatri of Bareilly) is fixed to be solemnised on the auspicious day of 9/9/20XX. You are humbly requested to bless the young couple.

Yours sincerely,
Ramdas Khatri

B-278, Ekta Apartment
Pashchim Vihar
New Delhi – 110063
R.S.V.P.

(Sample-21)

I feel honoured to inform Smt/Sri …that by the grace of God, the marriage of my younger brother Shiv Narain with Renu (D/O Sri Raja Ramji of Agra) is fixed to be solemnised on the auspicious day of 2.11/20XX. Please honour us, along with your children and grace the occasion by blessingt he young couple. The *barat* will leave by bus in the morning of 2/11/20XX.

Yours,
Krishna Nath Shastri

234, Gali Mirabai
Delhi - 110006
R.S.V.P.

(Sample-22)

I feel honoured to inform Smt/Sri ... that by the grace of God, the marriage of my son Anoop Singh with Shobna (D/O Sri Roop Narain Ji of Bareilly) is fixed to be solemnised on the auspicious day of 3/2/20XX. Please honour us, along with your children and grace the occasion as per the itinerary given in the invitation card.

(Barat will leave by train at 10.00 in the night of 2/2/20XX)

Yours truly,
Arjun Singh
Address

Dated...
R.S.V.P.

(Sample-23)
Invitation Accepted

Dear Arjunji!

We learnt with pleasure the news of the marriage of your son Anoop Singh with Shobna, D/O Sri Roop Narain Ji of Bareilly to be solemnised on the auspicious day of 3/2/20XX. We will definitely visit and bestow my blessings to Anoop. I had always looked forward to see this occasion fructify at the earliest.

Yours sincerely,
Kamal Kishore
Address

Dated...

(Sample-24)
Invitation Declined

Dear Arjunji!

    We learnt with pleasure the news of the marriage of your son Anoop Singh with Shobna, D/O Sri Roop Narain Ji of Bareilly to be solemnised on the auspicious day of 3/2/20XX. I had always looked forward to see this occasion fructify at the earliest. I regret I will not be able to be with you. The reason is somewhat disappointing and hence, I am not mentioning this at the moment. I am sending my best wishes for the young couple. I wish all the best for this marriage..

Yours truly,
Kamal Kishore
Address

Dated…

(Sample-25)
Postponement of Marriage

We regret to announce the marriage of Kumari Archana with Rakesh Kumar scheduled for 23rd June, 2012 has been postponed. Ashish, the younger brother of Archana met with an accident and expired. You will be informed in time as soon as a fresh date of marriage is finalised. We beg forgiveness for the unintended inconvenience.

Dated:

Vishwa Mohan
Address

(Sample-26)
Letters Sent Post-marriage

It is an Indian tradition that the bridegroom side presents gifts to the bride. This is usually given the name of 'Muh Dikhai". A letter conveying acceptance of the gift goes a long way in cementing the relationship.

This kind of letter is ordinarily written in the following way.

Dear Sadanandji!

It was very kind of you to have presented me a gift, which I very graciously accept. This is an invaluable presentation. I very much look forward to meet you in person in this new house of mine.

Yours truly,
Kanchan Kumari
Address

(Sample-27)

Dear Sir!

It"s kind of you to have thought of me to be deserving such a precious gift. It was really an honour. I look forward to meet you as a hostess of this new house of mine. I hope such an occasion would come soon.

Yours truly,
Kanchan Kumari
Address

(Sample-28)
Arranging a Tea Party to Introduce the Newlywed Couple

Smt. and Sri…are kindly requested to grace a tea-party organised at 'Sona & Roopa Restaurant" tomorrow dated 3rd February, 20XX at 5.00 in the evening. The party is intended to introduce Smt. Kavita Tilak, the newlywed wife of my bosom friend, Sri Ajay Tilakji among our close circle. We hope you would graciously join the function.

Dated:

Dinesh Kumar
Address

(Sample-29)
Acceptance of the Above

Dear Dineshji!

It is with pleasure that I received your invitation to attend a tea party to introduce Smt Kavita Tilak, the newlywed wife of Sri Ajay Tilakji among our close circle. I really felt honoured by this. At the appointed time, I would be there at Sona and Roopa restaurant to bless the young couple.

Dinesh Kumar
Address

Dated…

Invitation Letters

(Sample-30)
Declining the Above

Dear Dineshji!

It is with pleasure I received your invitation to attend a tea party to introduce Smt Kavita Tilak, the newlywed wife of Sri Ajay Tilakji among our close circle. I really felt honoured by this. I regret it will not be possible for me to attend the function since I am suffering from fever for the last four days.

I hope you will appreciate my inconvenience and excuse me.

Kindly bless the young couple on my behalf.

Your friend,
Rohit
Address

Dated...

(Sample-31)
Invitation on the Occasion of Birthday

Sri/Smt...Ji

By the grace of God, a baby boy was born to my son Anmol. On this occasion, a dinner party has been hosted at 6.00 in the evening on 19.2.20XX at my house. I hope to have the pleasure of having you to celebrate the birth of the boy.

Yours sincerely,
Gopal Mishra
Address

Dated...

(Sample-32)
Accepting the Above Invitation

Dear Mishraji,

    We all felt thrilled to hear the news of the birth of a baby boy to Anmol. God has bestowed an invaluable delight in the life of Anmol. God has also showered you a favour by granting your wish for which you had waited so long.

    I will find time soon to be with you all.

Your loving brother,
Amit Mishra
Address

Dated...

(Sample-33)
Declining the Above Invitation

Dear Mishraji,

    We received the invitation sent in the name of my parents. It was thrilling to hear the news of the birth of a baby boy to Anmol. It will not be possible for my parents to join you on this occasion since they have gone abroad on 8.2.20XX for about a month. I am conveying this news to them today itself.

    On behalf of my parents and myself, please accept our best wishes.

Your younger daughter,
Rajni
Address

Dated...

(Sample-34)
Invitation for Mundan Ceremony

Sri/Smt …Ji!

Ankur has completed two years and is stepping into his third year of life on Wednesday, 22.2.20XX. On this occasion, we have decided to organise a Mundan ceremony according to our Yagya Vidhi. Thereafter, dinner has also been scheduled.

Kindly make it convenient to bless the child.

Yours truly,
Saurabh Sharma
Address

Dated…

(Sample-35)
Acceptance of the Invitation for Mundan Ceremony

Dear Saurabhji!

The moment we received the invitation regarding Ankur"s second birthday and the coming Mundan ceremony, the memory of the invitation on his first birthday flashed across our minds vividly. That time he was lying on a swing and giving out gurgling smiles. I will surely join you on this occasion.

Yours truly,
Prem Prakash
Address

Dated…

(Sample-36)
Declining the Invitation for Mundan Ceremony

Dear Saurabhji!

    We received your invitation. That Ankur has completed two years and is moving into the third is a matter of great rejoice for all of us. We hope he keeps hale and hearty all through. We wanted to actively participate in the Mundan ceremony but for some unforeseen circumstances, it is just not possible to make a visit. We are sending our best wishes to Ankur.

Yours sincerely,
Prem Prakash
Address

Dated...

(Sample-37)
Invitation on the Death of Father

Dear friend,

    It is with a heavy heart, I have to inform you that my father left for his heavenly abode this morning at 5.35. I have lost him forever. I am totally shocked what to do. Now, it"s you and other close friends who will guide me in this difficult hour. I have decided to open a library in the name of my father. The *Rasam Pagdi* has been planned for 3.2.20XX. Kindly guide me and be with me in this hour of distress.

Yours sincerely,
Vinay Kumar
Address

Dated...

Invitation Letters

(Sample-38)
Accepting the Above Invitation

Dear Vinay,

    The sad news of the death of my Bhaiyya sent a shock wave through all of us here. Your *chachi* always regarded him as her elder brother. Tonight itself, I am catching a train to reach you. You are wise and intelligent and know how to conduct yourself in difficult circumstances. I hope you will bravely negotiate this difficult time. Please don"t despair. It"s time for you to console others. Be brave.

Your Uncle,
Suryamani
Address

Dated...

(Sample-39)
Declining the Above Invitation

Dear Vinay,

    The sad news of the death of your father sent a shock wave through all of us here. Heavy responsibility has fallen on your shoulder to console your bereaving family members and keep them intact. I regret, in the absence of my doctor"s advice, I can"t really take a chance to move out. I am sending your sister by train this evening itself. I will reach you as soon as I am in a position to move comfortably.

Yours truly,
Sheel Kumar
Address

Dated...

Letters of Sympathy

There are times when a person gets dejected, feels let down and doesn"t quite know what to do – not necessarily due to his fault, mistake or error of judgement. These are the times – hard times- when he yearns for words of sympathy and emotional support. It becomes the moral duty of friends and family members to go out and extend all possible assistance to prevent further deterioration in his mental outlook. A few examples of letters are written below.

(Sample-1)

A Letter of Sympathy

Address of the sender
Dated:

Dear Brother Ramesh,

Namaskar,

Today"s newspaper carried results the of your examination. I felt disappointed at not finding your name.

I need not mention that you must have felt the shock in equal measure, if not more. But then, please realise that life is composed of both ups and downs. Life goes on. It doesn"t stop. You have to get up, dust yourself and get going. This year, in particular, you didn"t keep good health, and lost three months due to sickness.

One suggestion though! If you are a little tired of Delhi at the moment, why don"t you come over to Shimla and spend some time here in altogether new surroundings away from the hustle and bustle of traffic, speed and noise. Your Bhabhi remembers you very much. Your nephew Kunnu also longs to be near you. He would be a plaything for you while keeping you company.

Yours affectionately,
Suresh

(Reply to the Above)

Address of the sender
Dated:

Dear Brother,
Namaskar,

    I am in receipt of your letter. No doubt, I failed but I am not the sort of person to lay prostrate in front of the failure. During three months of my sickness, I have completely revised the syllabus but then the culprit, 'sickness" didn"t spare me.

    Well! Whatever had to happen has happened. The plain fact is I am quite sick of the environment here. I am catching a train tomorrow to reach you. In the good company of children and Bhabhiji, I will be able to divert my attention and move on in life.

    Please convey my regards to Bhabhiji and love to children.

Yours affectionately,
Ramesh

(Sample-2)
On Losing a Football Match at School

Address of the sender
Dated:

Dear Baldev,

    I have come to know that our school team lost in the final of the football match by a slender goal. That apart, I am also told that your all-round display had sent shivers down the spine of the rival team. What I would like to stress is that this loss should cause you no worry and that such occasions keep cropping up every now and then. But the life goes on unmindful of what happened yesterday.

    I regret I couldn"t take the field due to my illness, but am proud of your field management.

    What significantly matters is, not the loss in the final, but the manner in which you carried the day, which in effect, translates into your personal victory.

    I hope you are not disappointed; and will look forward to leading the team with renewed vigour and vitality.

Your friend,
Raj

(Reply)

Address of the sender
Dated:

Dear Raj,

I received your letter. In your absence, it was very difficult to manage the show, but then we tried our best to take every match unitedly. We went right up to the final. Unfortunately, during the final match, my ankle twisted and the ball slipped through me into the goal line.

Now, we are focussing on the tournaments coming ahead. I hope, very soon, you will be joining us. Your absence has really handicapped us. Get well soon and join us to take our team ahead. God willing!

Your friend,
Baldev

(Sample-3)
Being Unsuccessful at a Competitive Examination

Address
Dated…

Dear Rajan,

I got a letter from Jeetendra this afternoon. It informed me of your failure to crack the examination held for the job. There is nothing to feel disheartened about. Success and failure are part of everyone"s life.

There is no point in rejoicing at success or showing despair at failure.

Initially, I could scarcely believe you were writing any competitive examination. I feel sure, this disappointment won"t hamper your ambition and would, in fact, propel you to constantly strive to move ahead in life.

Your friend,
Vinay

(Reply)

Address
Dated…

Dear Vinay,

I am in receipt of your letter. I am surely disappointed for failing to succeed at the examinations, but then I realise things like these go on. Your letter brought some solace, and comfort to me. In circumstances, such as this, only someone very close to you can fathom your feelings and touch the chord.

I know one day I would succeed.

Rest all is fine.

Your friend,
Rajan

(Sample -4)

Letter from a Father to his Son who has Lost his Job

Address
Dated…

My dear son,

Your mother tells me that by a letter, your wife has informed that for some unforeseen reason, you have been removed from the job. I can very well understand the sense of despondency you must be undergoing at the moment. But remember, life consists of both good and no-so-good times. The one who faces them squarely is the ultimate winner.

You are a son of a fearless father who has never bowed before any circumstances. I feel sure you would also come out unscathed. You have a solid character and I hope you will do nothing to impair that. Meanwhile, please come over to us for a change. In the meantime, we will try to get in touch with your senior officials to investigate the cause of your removal. Have no sense of fear or guilt.

Please come home soon.

Your father,
Vishwa Mohan

(Reply)

Address
Dated…

My dear father,

Your letter gave me a sense of comfort and well-being that I had lost for the past one week. That I lost the job is of little consequence, but what hurts me is my honesty, which was overlooked. Circumstances that floated before me could have made me millions, but my mind didn"t let me proceed. The result is there for you and I to see.

For quite some time, various kinds of insinuations and jibes were thrown at me but all of them remained unsuccessful. It was becoming increasingly difficult for me to adjust to the environment that prevailed here.

I have collected enough evidence to back my case. I have already written to the minister as well as to the secretary. They have assured me of looking into the case expeditiously. In case, nothing works, courts are the ultimate weapon of sorts. I am coming soon to discuss things over with you.

Your loving son,
Naresh

(Sample-5)
Factory Destroyed in Fire

Address
Dated…

Dear Pradeep,

It was highly disturbing to read in the newspaper the spate of fires occurring in factories in Delhi. It was emotionally painful to learn that your factory was also gutted in the inferno. I could scarcely visualise the memories of the large factory you had built.

The factory lives today in all, but memory and imagination. Nevertheless, I am sure, like the previous occasions where you had overcome many setbacks in the course of your business, you would succeed in rebuilding a still larger factory.

Please don"t hesitate to call me if you consider me worthy of any contribution.

Your friend,
Atma Dev

(Reply)

Address
Dated...

Dear Atma Devji!

I have received your emotionally charged letter today. You have lent me a crucial support at this juncture which will go a long way in lowering my difficulties. The fire was a real inferno that engulfed shops after shops in a large area. Along with mine, four other factories went into the flames completely. More than 500 workers lost their jobs and properties worth crores were destroyed by the fire.

Very few come forward to stand at times of real need. I won"t forget your strong feelings for me.

God is great. Nothing stands invincible before Him.

We have to learn to live with Him.

Your friend,
Pradeep

(Sample-6)
On Losing an Election

Address
Dated...

Dear Jai Prakashji!

I was painful to hear of the election result of your constituency. It is a matter of regret that the voters have chosen to send your rival Sri Ram Dayal Ji to parliament as their representative instead of a genuine worker like yourself. Except for raising his hand in support or otherwise of any issue, he would hardly do anything else.

The voters are illiterate and because of this, they send representatives like Sri Ram Dayal Ji. It matters little for dedicated people like you to officially represent any constituency. Work is worship for you. I am sure you would hardly care for this result.

Yours sincerely,
Ramanuj

(Reply)

Address
Dated…

Dear Ramanujji!

    I received your letter of sympathy. Winning or losing are just the two possible outcomes of any election. If not a victory, losing is the only alternative. I wanted to go to parliament for a certain cause.

    I would have represented that cause in particular. I am a dedicated soldier and am not afraid of anything.

    I know many more such occasions would come in future. I know I can rely on friends like you.

Yours sincerely,
Jai Prakash

(Sample-7)
On Being Attacked

Address
Dated…

Dear Suryabhanji!

    Just now I learnt from Atmanand that some miscreants attacked you at night the day before yesterday due to which you suffered injuries in your hands and legs. It was quite painful to hear this dastardly attack. I guess these people are the same with whom you have a long running court case. It is shocking that they attacked a person while asleep.

    If there is anything I could do, please don"t hesitate to call me. I would immediately rush. Right now, I couldn"t make it to you because my son is very ill. I would reach you as soon as he recovers from his illness.

Yours,
Jai Prakash

(Reply)

Address
Dated…

Dear Raghunandanji!

I received your letter just now. I have received letters of sympathy from all those who heard this. Anyway, whatever had to happen has happened. Nothing could be done about this. You may be pleased to know that I fought four of the miscreants single-handedly. You may be right in guessing that these hired goons were sent by the person with whom I have an account case running for long.

I have not really suffered much. Kindly convey my regards to Bhabhiji and inform her that there is nothing to worry. I thank you for enquiring about my welfare.

If there is anything I could do, please don"t hesitate to call me. I would immediately rush and be at your service at the earliest.

Yours,
Suryabhan

(Sample-8)
Theft in the House

Address
Dated…

Dear Jijaji!

I received the sad news through Didi"s letter just now. I was stunned to hear of the theft committed in the house. For a moment, I failed to apprehend what"s happened.

Jija Ji, you are elder to me, so for me to discourse you on patience and forbearance looks inappropriate. Nevertheless, to regret what has already been done makes little justice and a waste of time.

Please don"t hesitate to ask me to do anything you believe I am capable of as I am always ready. I am leaving by train tomorrow to reach you. Kindly console Didi on this unfortunate account.

Yours,
Kumar

(Sample-9)

On Losing an Election

Address
Dated…

Dear Harsh!

    I came to know through Surendra Mohan that you have lost the court case. It"s very painful. But then, the brave never fear the loss and remain unperturbed. I am sure this loss will not have much effect on you. You have won as well as lost umpteen cases like this one. I am of the opinion that you should file a case in the Supreme Court. It"s quite possible; the lower court"s decision could be set aside. From my side, I would strive hard to use my resources to the maximum possible extent. Please try to get over this loss.

Yours sincerely,
Shashibhushan

(Reply to the Above)

Address
Dated…

Dear Shashibhushan!

    I received your letter and felt quite relieved. This particular case consumed three precious years. And the outcome was zero. The matter stayed where it was. Time, money and energy all gone down the drain.

    What I am really worried is not the loss of money, time or energy but the honour and name and fame. I will consider your opinion and appeal in the Supreme Court. Let"s see the outcome there. Our job is to do our bit and hope for the best. I am coming to Delhi to offer my support and guidance.

Your younger brother,
Harsh

(Sample-10)

Letters of Sympathy

On the Death of a Close Relative

                                                                                                           Address
                                                                                                            Dated...

Dear Purushottam Prasadji!

    It was painful to hear from Jeevan Lal Ji that your brother Sri Dushyant Ji expired at 12 in the afternoon yesterday. It is an irreparable loss to your family. It is difficult to recount the number of occasions Dushyant Ji had pulled the family out of hard times. In fact, you never really had to worry as long as he was alive. Now the responsibility squarely rests on your head. I hope you will do your best as far as taking care of them is concerned.

    Please don"t hesitate to call me for whatever worth you consider me. May God help him rest in peace and allow Bhabhiji and her children to forebear the loss.

                                                                                                                Your friend,
                                                                                                                  Rajpal

(Reply to the Above)

                                                                                                                Address
                                                                                                                Dated...

Dear Rajpal!

    I am grateful to you for sending me your sympathies. The untimely demise of my dear brother has really sucked the strength out of me. While he was alive, I was having a smooth and uninterrupted life. He was shouldering the complete responsibility of the family. I was never required to worry about anything.

    Now suddenly, the responsibility has fallen on my shoulders. I hope he will continue to guide us from where he resides in heaven. I am sure, with people like you around, I will have every kind of support whenever needed.

    I have not been able to send a prompt and coherent reply due to my current state of mind. I hope you will forgive me for this.

                                                                                             Your friend,
                                                                                      Purushottam Prasad

Congratulatory Letters

Occasions arise when we feel like congratulating someone on achieving something remarkable.

Given below are a few examples of messages sent on different occasions.

(Sample-1)

Congratulatory Letter on the Publication of a Magazine

Name and address of the sender
Date…

Dear Dr.Vaibhavji,

    Hearty congratulations!

    I received you letter and learnt of the successful publication of the magazine, 'Jan Bharti". As I was out of town, I regret that I couldn"t reply earlier.

    I wish you all the best in your farsighted effort in publishing a magazine that reflects the current thoughts on literature, culture and the national ideals. Please accept my wishes once again!

    Regards,

Yours affectionately,
Prem Prakash

(Sample-2)

Congratulating a Friend on Topping the B.A. Exams and Getting Honoured with Gold Medal

Dear Ravi,

Many congratulations!

It was pleasure no end for me on learning that not just the college, you have topped the Mumbai University in the recently held B.A. examinations. That Mumbai University chose to honour you with the Gold Medal has sent me soaring into the seventh heaven. I am short of words and just don"t know how to express my heart-felt emotions. Please accept my best wishes! It was made possible because of your single-handed effort and devotion; apart from your equally sound activities at games and sports.

I strongly feel that likewise you will achieve an identical result in your M.A. examinations and make your parents proud. I wish you continue on this path of success in all your future endeavours. My parents are sending their best wishes for you.

Please convey my regards to your parents and love to your younger brother, Rohan.

Yours affectionately,
Manoj

(Sample-3)

Congratulating a Friend on Getting a Ph.D Degree

Name and address of the sender
Dated...

Dear Vijaykantji,

Warm greetings!

It gave me immense pleasure to learn that the Delhi University has honoured you with the degree of a Ph.D (Name of the subject). My sincere congratulations to you on this remarkable achievement!

I wish you achieve innumerable such successes in life!

Yours truly,
Narendra Rajput

(Sample-4)
Greeting on the Birthday of a Friend

Name and address of the sender
Dated…

Dear Ashok,

    Warm greetings!

    I received your birthday invitation card. Thank you for the same. I always grow impatient for your birthday as soon as January gets near. It is nearly impossible to forget birthdays of friends like you.

    I am afraid I will not be able to join the birthday celebrations this time because my mother is due for an eye operation. There is none to take care of her. In case, my father gets leave from the office, I would certainly join you all.

    I wish, every moment of life bestows you happiness and pleasure. On your birthday, I am sending you a few books on literature and a camera. I hope you will like them.

    Congratulations from my side again.

    Please convey my regards to your parents and love to youngsters.

    Best wishes!

Your friend,
Vijayendra

(Sample-5)
Congratulatory Letter on Winning an Election

Name and address of the sender
Dated…

Dear Swaroopchandji,

    Warm greetings!

    Congratulations on winning the seat in the Uttar Pradesh Vidhan Sabha election by the highest margin.

    I hope the condition prevailing in the State will improve and the development works taken in the right earnest.

Yours truly,
Devesh

(Sample-6)
Congratulatory Letter on Being Appointed as a Lecturer

Name and address of the sender
Dated…

Dear Rajesh,

Warm greetings!

I received your letter today. It gave me a great pleasure to learn that you have been appointed as a lecturer in English in the prestigious Pune"s College of Arts and Commerce. My parents felt hugely exhilarated on hearing this news. Congratulations once again!

Please treat the students in a friendly manner. Your sincerity will take you a long way in pursuit of a great career.

Yours truly,
Anand Kumar

(Sample-7)
Congratulations on Winning a Lottery

Name and address of the sender
Dated…

Dear Jayant,

Your family members informed me that you have won a lottery for ₹ 10 lakh last week. Initially, it was hard to believe, but when your mother showed me your letter regarding this, then I was able to believe. Congratulations to you again!

Now I realise that it is possible to win a dream by spending a rupee or two. I had heard about lottery winners before, but it"s the first time someone close to me has actually won it. I have also come to believe that lotteries are run fairly.

Goddess Lakshmi bestows her rewards to honest people like you only. You may have seen many people going bust in search of becoming a *lakhpati* by any means- fair or foul.

I hope after taking care of your household, you would contribute some of the amount towards the national fund for earthquake victims.

Everyone here is fine. Convey my regards to Bhabhiji and love to Armaan.

Yours sincerely,
Akash

(Sample-8)
Congratulations on the Birth of a Baby Boy/Girl

Name and address of the sender
Dated…

Dear Bhabhiji,

Ramesh bhaiyya informed us that you have given birth to a baby boy. We felt overjoyed with this news. Ammaji and Babuji are also extremely happy. Many congratulations to you and the young one! My mother is quite anxious to see the baby.

Kindly pay our regards to your parents and love to the youngsters in the family. This Sunday, I am coming there along with my mother.

Rest all is fine.

Yours affectionately,
Sachin

(Sample-9)
Congratulations on the Publication of a Novel

Name and address of the sender
Dated…

Dear Sagarji,

I received your letter dated… I couldn"t reply earlier because of certain important engagement. It"s a matter of pleasure that your novel, 'Arunima" has come out of print.

Your contribution for the literature, culture and national integration is truly worthwhile and appreciable.

Kindly accept my congratulations once again.

Yours sincerely,
Utkarsh Tiwari

(Sample-10)
Congratulations on Being Appointed as a Special Executive Officer

Name and address of the sender
Dated…

Dear Swadeshji,

It is a great news to hear that the Delhi government has appointed you as a Special Executive Officer. Congratulations on this happy news.

I hope you are keeping well.

Yours sincerely,
Sagar Sinha

(Sample-11)
Forms of Greetings on Diwali

Best wishes on the auspicious occasion of Diwali!
May you live your life like the glittering festival of Diwali, happy healthy and wealthy!
A Very Very Happy Diwali!
Diwali night is full of lights, may your life be filled with colours and lights of happiness.
Happy Diwali!
May this Diwali be as bright as ever!
May this Diwali bring joy, health and prosperity to you!
May the festival of lights brighten you and your near and dear ones" lives!
May this Diwali bring in you the brightest and choicest happiness and love you have ever wished for!
May this Diwali bring you the utmost in peace and prosperity!
May lights triumph over darkness!
May the spirit of light illuminate your world!
May the light that we celebrate at Diwali show us the way and lead us together on the path of peace and social harmony!
'WISH YOU A VERY HAPPY DIWALI"!

(Sample-12)
New Year Greetings

Here comes the new ones that will bring you cheer; Forget the past, the future is here; Let us welcome the Happy New Year!
Sending you the warmest hugs of the season… and wishing you the best of times.
Happy New Year!
So many ways to greet you Happy New Year, but I reserve the most special one to you. I love you anytime of the year.
Happy New Year!
Each moment in a day has its own value. Morning brings HOPE, Afternoon brings FAITH, Evening brings LOVE, Night brings REST, Hope you will have all of them every day. HAPPY NEW YEAR!
A New Year starts, with a new calendar. But my love stays constant, with you always in my heart. Happy New Year!
Wishing you all the blessings of the New Year...the warmth of home, the love of family and the company of good friends!
Happy New Year to all!
Let us greet the New Year with the hope that it will be a better year for all of us!
Happy New Year!
May God continue to bless you and your family with the divine light, love and power that will bring much love, joy, peace, inner strength and overflowing abundance in your home!
Happy New Year!
A blessed & joyous New Year to you and your family!
May the Goddess continue to bless you and your family with the things that matter most in life - a gift of good health, happy home and peace of mind throughout the coming year!
Happy New Year!
12 months have passed, and another 12 will come, but my memory of you remains constant in my mind. Happy New Year my love!
Sunrise makes our mornings beautiful and makes our lives more meaningful.
Happy New Year!
Keep the smile, Leave the tear, Think of joy, Forget the fear, Hold the laugh, Leave the pain, Be joyous! Because it"s New Year!
Happy New Year!

(Sample-13)
Birthday Greetings

Warm wishes on your birthday!
Many happy returns of the day! Happy Birthday!
You will soon start a new phase of life! But that can wait until you are older. Enjoy another year of being young.
Happy Birthday!
I hope that today is the beginning of a great year for you.
Happy Birthday!
Happy Birthday! Have a wonderful happy, healthy birthday and many more to come.
You have a birthday twinkle in your eye so have fun and know we love you fairly much.
Happy Birthday!
Things I like about you: humour, looks, everything.
Happy Birthday!
I love celebrating with you. Thanks for having a birthday and giving us a reason.
Happy Birthday!
I wish you a great and wonderful Happy Birthday!! I hope you have an amazing day and lots of fun! Enjoy this day, you deserve it!
Hope your day is simply terrific!
Happy Birthday!
Wishing you a spectacularly beautiful birthday!
Happy Birthday!
Wishing you tons of happiness on your birthday!
Enjoy it!
Wishing you love and happiness on your birthday!
Happy Birthday!

(Sample-14)
Responding to a Congratulatory Message

Address:
Dated:

Dear Jijaji,

Saadar Pranam!

Many thanks for the mail and the parcel. I was simply delighted to see the gift.

I just fail to understand, how to reciprocate your feelings of love.

You know for sure my love for photography. The look of the wrist watch and camera are beyond words. I am getting used to wearing this watch and constantly looking for time. The camera is a world unto itself- great to capture images of tourist spots, birthday snaps, etc. I will be able to preserve memories for long with the help of the camera.

I once again thank you for the superb gifts you have sent me. Convey my regards to Didiji and love to Armaan, Muskan and Naisha.

Yours affectionately,
Shubham

Regret Letters

(Sample-1)
Regretting Failure to Submit an Article for the Magazine

Name and address of the sender
Dated:

Dear Shiv Mohanji,

I am grateful to you for your mail. It gives me a great pleasure to learn that you are about to bring out the second edition of the magazine, 'Sahitya Agraj".

Please accept my best wishes.

I regret I am unable to contribute any article due to my hectic schedule and my failing health.

I hope you will accept my apology.

Thanking you,

Yours sincerely,
Sooraj Prakash

(Sample-2)
Inability to Attend a Marriage Function

Name and address of the sender
Dated:

Dear Kartikeya,

Thank you for the card inviting me to attend the marriage function. My warmest greetings on the occasion of marriage!

Actually, I had a great desire to attend the function and believed that it would offer me an opportunity to meet my friends of many years.

I regret the marriage day clashed with the date my father was scheduled to undergo a bypass surgery. My presence at the hospital was necessitated all the more because I am the lone child of my parents and there"s none to take care of.

Despite my longing to be with you, it just couldn"t materialise. You understand the predicament I was in at that time.

I am looking forward to meet you and my dear Bhabhi at the first opportunity that comes my way. Please convey my regards to Bhabhi and respect to the elders and love to all the young ones in the family.

I trust you all are keeping well.

Your friend,
Yogesh

(Sample-3)
Seeking Excuse for Not Reaching on the Demise of Friend"s Father

Name and address of the sender
Dated:

Dear Bhupendra,

I received the painful news of the sad demise of your father. He was loved by one and all. Living for others seemed to be his motto. I don"t remember ever seeing him in a furious mood.

I wanted to take part in the last rites but simply couldn"t do so because my son fell ill around the same time. I hope you will forgive me for this absence.

I will surely be there on the Terahvi".

Your friend,

Rakesh

(Sample-4)
Seeking Excuse for Not Reaching the Kavya Sammelan

Name and address of the sender
Dated:

Dear Siddhant,

I regret to inform you that on..., I will not be able to reach Kamani Auditorium at witness you reciting poems during the Kavya Sammelan. The reason being that on date day itself, I have to go out of an official work.

I hope you will be kind enough to excuse me.

Your friend,
Abhinandan

(Sample-5)
Letter to Father Seeking Excuse for Falling into Bad Company

Name and address of the sender
Dated:

Dear father,

I understand you have received a letter from our principal. It must have been painful to you. Through this letter, I want to clarify the issue.

Please understand that prior to the incident; I was unaware that Dinesh and Nitin undulge in petty thefts from shops. Last Saturday, they asked me to accompany them to the lake. I agreed. Pretending some urgent work, Dinesh didn"t come along for boating. Nitin and I enjoyed about half an hour of boating in the lake. While returning, Nitin went and sat in a taxi. I felt uncomfortable when the taxi started moving towards Kathgodam. On being asked, they said we will go to Delhi. I couldn"t do anything but upon reaching Kathgodam, I made an excuse to call on the nature, I got down, took a lift from a tourist and returned back to Nainital.

Around midnight, I informed the hostel warden who later informed the police. Next day, the police arrested them in Delhi. I beg your forgiveness for my foolishness to be their friends. It won"t happen again in life.

Kindly forgive me and give another chance.

Regards,

Your loving son,
Sarthak Kumar

Letter of Recommendation

(Sample-1)

Introducing a Friend to a Publisher for Publishing his/her Manuscript

Dear Anujji,

I trust this finds you in cheers. For quite some time, I have not received your letter. You are an old hat at not writing letters, nevertheless, there wouldn"t be any disaster, if you write one once in a while.

Sudhanshu Ji who is before you is an old friend of mine – very close, very intimate. He is well versed and equally adept both in writing poems and prose. A number of his books have been published.

Right at the moment, he has approached you with a manuscript – a novel. It has critically analysed the burning problems razing the society currently.

I hope and wish, you will publish his work that he has penned with great diligence.

Yours sincerely,
Vinayak
Address

Dated:

(Affirmative Reply to the Above)

Dear Vinayakji,

Sudhanshuji has handed over your letter to me. I have received the Novel. These days we are not publishing novels but since it"s your wish, we will publish the same.

I regret the delay in replying in time.

Yours friend,
Anuj
Address

Dated…

(Letter of Regret)

Dear Vinayakji,

Sudhanshuji has handed over your letter to me. It would have been pleasing if we could publish the same. Since the last month, my elder brother has taken charge of the publication business. I am in charge of only the press section.

I hope you will appreciate the inconvenience I am feeling in not honouring your word and excuse me for the same.

Rest all is fine.

Yours friend,
Anuj
Address

Dated...

(Sample-2)
Recommending a Known Person for a Job

Dear Prabhakar,

It was pleasing to hear from a machineman, Shyam Singh that your Mansarovar Press is one of the best known presses in Delhi. Shyam Singh is the person carrying this letter to you. He is a dedicated person and is highly duty-bound. He just keeps himself to the job at hand and doesn"t waste time in anything else.

Shyam Singh has worked for us for nearly seven years. During this period, he never gave any opportunity for any complaint. I have come to know that there is a vacancy for a suitable machineman in your press. If you need such a dedicated person, you may hire him.

Please write to me if there is anything I could do for you.

Yours friend,
Virendra
Address

Dated...

(Affirmative Response)

Dear Virendra,

    Shyam Singh has given me your letter. What you have written about the successful running of the press is due to well-wishers like you only. A few days ago, I have installed two new presses and for that I need two competent people. In this respect, I had inserted advertisements in *The Times of India* and *Hindustan Times*.

    I am already aware of the ability of Shyam Singh. I am much impressed with the books printed in your press. You have greatly eased my problem by recommending an outstanding worker to me.

    I have hired Shyam Singh at a salary of ₹ 8,000 per month.

    Do let me know if there is anything worthwhile for me to do.

Yours friend,
Prabhakar
Address

Dated…

(Negative Response)

Dear Virendra,

    Shyam Singh has given me your letter. The successful running of my press is due to well-wishers like you only. This month I have installed two new presses and for that I needed two competent people. In this respect, I had inserted advertisements in *The Times of India* and *Hindustan Times*. In response, I have only yesterday appointed two machine men.

    I wish Shyam Singh had come with your letter yesterday. It would have been my pleasure in appointing him. I feel extremely sorry in not being able to carry out your recommendation. However, I have requested Shyam Singh to keep in touch with me. One never knows when opportunity strikes.

    Do let me know if there is anything worthwhile for me to do.

Yours friend,
Prabhakar
Address

Dated…

Letter of Recommendation

(Sample-3)
Recommending a Suitable Person for a Job

Dear Sri Omkar Nathji,

I have come to know that you are working towards opening an NGO (Non-government Organisation) in Bareilly and are in search of a dedicated person to run it efficiently.

A few days back, one of my close friends, Chitraguptaji had come from Benares. He is one of the gems who has dedicated his services for the cause of the society. During discussions with him, I gathered that he is looking out for a base to further the areas of social activities to reach across more needy persons. I believe, if he joins hands with you, his services will help you serve people the way you cherish.

Chitraguptaji is a person, our nation should be proud of. Sincerity, sense of dedication and diligence are the hallmark of his life.

You have adequate funds at your disposal. If he gets a chance to join you, the society will be immensely benefitted.

Kindly inform me by the return of mail, if I should extend him the proposal.

Yours friend,
Som Dutt Narayan
Address

Dated...

(Affirmative Reply to the Above)

Dear Som Duttji,

I have received your mail. By informing me about Chitraguptaji and his ability to run the NGO, you have taken a huge load off my back. I have already opened the NGO, but lack of suitable persons to run it efficiently continues to worry me. I warmly welcome your suggestion. And hope you will promptly invite Chandraguptaji at the earliest so that the job could be entrusted to him.

I would be ever grateful to you for this act.

Yours friend,
Omkar Nath
Address

Dated...

(Negative Reply)

Dear Som Duttji,

 I have received your mail. I have no reason to doubt your opinion about Chitraguptaji. But I regret, I am not in a position to assign work to him at the moment. Currently, Brahmachari Sadanandji is efficiently running the job. You would be pleased to know that within a short time, he has been able to do a lot.

 I hope this letter keeps you informed and that it won"t be a source of inconvenience to you.

Yours friend,
Omkar Nath
Address

Dated...

Letters Expressing Obligation

Often times, we feel obliged to express our gratitude to someone – friends, relatives, high functionaries or some individuals- for their actions that has helped us in one or more ways. Such letters fall under the heading *individual or public obligatory letters.*

(Sample-1)
Letter Expressing Obligation to an Individual

Name and address of the sender
Dated:

Dear Sir,

Warm greetings!

I am delighted to hear that my son Abhinav has topped his class. I agree he is intelligent and dedicated but I singularly attribute his success to your style and method of teaching. That he would gain immensely under your guidance was something I was pretty sure right from the beginning.

I am heavily indebted to you for the confidence you have reposed in him and placed him where he is today.

I am immensely grateful to you.

Please accept my best regards.

Yours faithfully,
Pyare Lal

(Reply to the Above)

Dear Pyare Lalji,

I am thrilled to receive your best wishes. To have Abhinav in my class was one of the most remarkable moments in my teaching career. It is true, as a teacher, we pay attention in equal measure to all the students, A few of them intelligently imbibe our dedication to teaching and achieve success, while other subdued ones fail to move along despite repetitive lectures.

Abhinav has truly made us proud in all respects. The crown of success rightly goes to Abhinav; besides the parents whose upbringing made him a star beyond compare!

Yours sincerely,
Nand Lal
Principal, Hindi Vidyalaya

(Sample-2)

Name and address of the sender
Dated…

Dear Vidyaji,

Pranam!

    I am at a loss of words to express my gratitude to you. Every single strand of my body is obliged to you. You have given me a new lease of life. Not only I, but the whole family is grateful to your benevolence. I will constantly look to be of some use to you, if ever the need arises.

Yours faithfully,
Nardev Dev

(Reply to the Above)

Name and address of the sender
Dated…

Dear Nardevji,

Pranam!

    Thank you for your kind letter. I am pleased to know that you are absolutely hale and hearty. In fact, your problem was old and chronic. That the medicines have helped you to get over the painful disease has given us confidence in the efficacy of our system of treatment.

    In fact, there is no reason for you to be grateful to us. It"s our basic duty. All I have done is to perform my duty.

Yours faithfully,
Ram Mani Vaidya

(Sample-3)

Name and address of the sender
Dated...

Dear Didi,

Pranam!

The kind of financial help extended to me is something I would never forget. I am truly obliged to you and Jijaji. It"s only due to your effort that my family could be resurrected. The business is progressing smoothly. I hope in the foreseeable future, I will be in a position to return the loan without any difficulty.

Rest all is fine.

Yours younger brother,
Sandeep

(Reply to the Above)

Name and address of the sender
Dated...

Dear Sandeep,

Love!

The kind of letter you have written has hurt us. Your Jijaji is equally sad. You were very young when you came under our care following the death of our mother. Both of us treated you like a child. I fail to understand how you summoned the courage to write such a letter.

Please don"t repeat this in future.

Yours sister,
Rajni

(Sample-1)
Obligatory Letters

Name and address of the sender
Dated...

The Director,
Education Department
Uttar Pradesh

Dear Sir,

    Humbly I wish to state that by appointing me to the vacant post lying under your control, you have done a yeoman"s service to our whole family.

    For this, I will ever remain grateful to you.

Yours faithfully,
Surya Pratap Singh

(Sample-2)

Name and address of the sender
Dated...

Dear Sir,

    All the members of my family are grateful to you for saving our lives from fire. It was sheer providence that you were around. Otherwise, the restricted road space of the locality would have prevented fire tenders from reaching the area under fire. We are short of words to thank you.

    We would be pleased to be of some service to you.

Yours faithfully,
Jeevan Prakash

(Sample-3)

Name and address of the sender
Dated…

Dear Sir,

    I am at a loss for words to express my gratitude to you for saving the life of my lone child unscathed out of the brutal fire that had engulfed the area. You have done what I couldn"t do as a father. People like you are rare who are prepared to sacrifice their comfort for the sake of others.

    I would be much obliged if I could be of some use to you now or ever.

Yours sincerely,
Navin

(Sample-4)

Social Obligatory Letter

Name and address of the sender
Dated…

Dear Sri Kumar Gandharvaji,

    Your classical music floored the residents of Delhi. It"s something people will recite for long. India truly feels proud of your achievement. You have taken the Indian Art to a height never achieved before.

    On behalf of all of Delhi, I extend our warmest thanks to you. I hope we all will relish and cherish the melodious recital for long.

On behalf of the citizens of Delhi,
Madan Mohan Mehta

(Sample-5)

Name and address of the sender
Dated…

Dear Madan Mohanji,

I am grateful for your kind letter. The recital which you, on behalf of the Delhi residents have appreciated and respectfully spoken is, in fact, one of the art form of India since ancient times. I am simply a practitioner of this art.

I feel personally obliged to you all for showering such a high regard. It would be remarkably wonderful if I get another opportunity to recite before the knowledgeable and appreciative people that the citizens of Delhi are known for.

Your sincerely,
Kumar Gandharva

(Sample-6)

Name and address of the sender
Dated…

Dear Acharyaji,

You have done a great service to the Hindi literature by wrting a history of Hindi Literature. No doubt, the history of Hindi literature written by Acharya Ramchandra Shukla is immortal but we have to appreciate that the subject of history is moving at a rapid pace. Today"s news becomes stale tomorrow. Hence, there is a growing need to rewrite and reflect the current history in the right perspective. You have done a brilliant job. On behalf of the lovers of Hindi, I am sending you a congratulatory letter.

I hope you would graciously accept our regards,

Yours sincerely,
Dinanath Bhargava

Letters Expressing Obligation

(Sample-7)
(Reply)

Name and address of the sender
Dated...

Dear Bhargavaji,

I am in receipt of your kind letter. The manner in which you have accepted my manuscript is a matter of great rejoice for me. I see no reason why you should be so grateful. As a matter of fact, I am just doing what I am expected to do as a writer. I am just serving the cause of Hindi literature.

Yours sincerely,
Dhirendra Prasad

(Sample-8)
(Reply)

Name and address of the sender
Dated...

Dear Sir,

Yesterday, I saw the working of your newly manufactured knitting machine at a factory. A designer cloth piece was being weaved on it. This kind of machine is going to help India manufacture some outstanding materials. I offer my sincere gratitude to you on behalf of the citizens of Palampur.

Yours sincerely,
Beni Madhav

(Sample-9)
(Reply)

Name and address of the sender
Dated...

Dear Beni Madhavji,

    I am grateful for the appreciation you have shown. This machine has been designed basically for the propagation and working in rural areas. We hope weavers in rural areas would be benefitted immensely by working on it.

Yours sincerely,
D. Divakar

(Sample-10)

Name and address of the sender
Dated...

Dear Kamalji,

    I hope you all are hale and hearty. The kind of service you have showered on people of this area during your three years of stay is simply outstanding. I am sure you will continue to extend your best wherever you go and live. I hope you will continue to guide us with your valuable suggestion at all times.

Yours sincerely,
Srinivas
Convenor,
District Congress Committee

(Reply)

Name and address of the sender
Dated…

Dear Srinivasji,

    I am thankful to you for your kind letter. During my three years of living with good people like you has strengthened our relationship to such an extent that I wouldn"t be able to forget it even if I wish to. The love extended by people of your area is beyond expression in words.

    I hope you and I will continue to have a cordial relationship as we had althrough.

Yours faithfully,
Kamal
Address

Date…

Letters of Obligation, Condolence, etc.

(Sample-1)
A Thank You Letter for Donating Books for the Library

Name and address of the sender
Dated:

Dear Dr. Kailashji,

We are grateful to you for donating our library a few rare books on Hindi literature. These books are generally not available in the market.

We are sure many readers who are desirous of reading these books would be greatly benefitted.

We value your contribution from the bottom of our hearts.

Regards,

Yours sincerely,
Anant 'Agaman"

(Sample-2)
Thanking a Person for Returning the Lost Papers

Name and address of the sender
Dated:

Dear Sri Mishraji,

When I placed an advertisement in the newspaper under the 'lost" column, I had hardly expected to get the papers back. Right now, when I got them back under an envelope, I was delightfully surprised. Although, we have never met, I get the feeling as if my elder brother is returning the same to me, while cautioning me to be more careful in future. We are totally at a loss when we discovered its loss during our bus journey. The papers included some important documents of my father besides other certificates. By promptly returning them, you have really won our hearts.

I have no words to express my gratitude. I am highly obliged to you and would certainly like to meet you whenever you have time. I look forward to meeting you soon.

Yours sincerely,
Chetan Singh

(Sample-3)
Condolence Letter to a Friend on the Death of his Mother

Name and address of the sender
Dated:

Dear Anil,

    We all were stunned to hear the sudden demise of your mother. We had expected her to enjoy life for many more years. But then, who has control over destiny? Anyone who has come is destined to go one day. May God give you the strength to bear this irreparable loss! The whole village folks would feel the void caused by her absence. We can replace everything but our parents! Please take care to fulfil the wishes of your mother. Only that would be the best form towards your attempts to repay her debt, if that could be said.

    May God let her soul rest in peace!

Your friend,
Karan Sood

(Sample-4)
Condolence Letter to a Friend on the Death of his Father

Name and address of the sender
Dated:

Dear Satishji,

    We all were shocked to hear the sad news of the sudden demise of your father. It was hard to believe it happened so unexpectedly. We are at a loss for words to express our sense of pain. We are all insignificant in front of the Almighty. In such a situation, there is little anyone could do. Now, the entire responsibility has fallen on your shoulders. I hope you will be able to squarely meet them.

    We were a close-knit member of the family. His sublime guidance was always available to us.

    I pray to God to let his soul rest in peace and give you the strength to bear this irreparable loss.

Your friend,
Aman Kumar

(Sample-5)
Condolence Letter to a Friend on the Death of his Father

Name and address of the sender
Dated:

Dear Ajay,

My heart sank to hear the news of the sudden demise of your father this afternoon. It was really hard to believe it happened so unexpectedly. Just the last week when I was with you all, he conversed with me in an intimate tone and voice as if I was a close-knit member of the family. Truly, he was an epitome of love! His sublime nature and effervescence is hard to replicate.

It is true, time and tide wait for none. Death is beyond our control. It is destiny; one who has come is bound to go some day. Only difference is that some depart early while others wait a little longer.

Kindly gather the courage to bestow strength to your mother and little sister to bear this great loss. May God give each one of you strength to overcome the hard times; and peace to the departed soul!

I hope to reach your house soon.

Your friend,
Bhuvan

(Sample-6)
Condolence Message

With a heavy heart, we inform you the untimely demise of our father, Dayanand Sharma on…

To perform the necessary rites for the departed soul, a meeting has been arranged at our house on Monday, dated…….. from 9 – 11 in the morning and 4 – 6 in the evening.

Address
Residence

Surya Sharma
Aditya Sharma
Abhinav Sharma, and
the Sharma Family

Descriptive Letters

Now let us have a look at some of the personal letters. In this section, we will pay attention to only those letters which a person writes to his relatives or friends. These letters enquire about personal and family welfare. They don"t talk about commercial matters. The subject matter of these letters come from the heart and are broadly of four kinds. These are Descriptive, Emotional, Travel-related and General.

(Sample-1)
Descriptive Letters

Dear Rajni,

I trust mummy, papa and all the youngsters in the family are hale and hearty.

Ever since the time I read the glory of Taj Mahal, it has been my earnest desire to have a close look at this monument. I did decide to go to Agra many times, but the plan kept getting dropped for one reason or the other. Finally, I got an opportunity to visit Agra along with my school friends.

Taj Mahal occupies a unique place among the great monuments of the world. It represents symbolically the emotional integration of love and affection best reflected in the moonlit night. Many lovebirds profess their love for one another here in the surroundings of the beautiful Taj for all times to come.

The foreigners who visit India always try to fit-in and ensure to pay a visit to this great marvel of the Mughal architecture. This mausoleum built by Shah Jahan in memory of his beloved wife Mumtaz Mahal took more than 20 years to be built at an enormous cost of crores of rupees. This was built during the time of the great famine and its construction enabled many distressed hands to earn a living. The materials used were expensive white marbles and precious gems and stones cut to proper sizes.

Agra is situated on the bank of the River Yamuna. It flows from its rear side. The moment I entered the huge gate of the Taj Mahal, I was standing right in front of the the epoch-making monument of love that Shah Jahan had built. There were rows of trees lined up right from the gate till the monument"s entrance. Fountains enhanced the beauty.

We reached the monument and were literally blinded with its breath-taking white marbled setting. Tall minarets were erected at the four corners of the white marble-made square platform. A few went atop the minaret and had a panoramic view. The architecture simply left us wonderstruck.

Dear Rajni, what do I tell you about the art and craft on the monument and the minarets? I am absolutely at a loss for words. Eye-soothing paintings made it difficult to differentiate between the original and the fake ones. In the centre of the mausoleum, two graves have been built in memory of the great Mughal emperor Shah Jahan and his beloved Mumtaz. It is the place where lies, in eternity, the souls of the two great lovers.

Today happened to be the full moon day. I realise that the beauty of the Taj Mahal will stand in full glory for years to come. A few foreigners were also there who were nonplussed with its beauty as much as we were.

I wish you were also with me along with mummy. We all would have enjoyed the phenomenal beauty all the more. I hope to bring you along to visit Taj Mahal during this summer vacation.

Your loving brother,
Sagar

Agra
Dated:

(Sample-2)

Letter to a Younger Brother Suggesting Ways to Stay Healthy

Address:
Date:...............

Dear Sushil

Trust this finds you in cheers. I have received a letter from our mother. She is worried about your health. I know mothers are quite sentimental and worry about even small things. But there are some facts that do cause genuine worry. So I thought I should speak to you on this matter. Pay attention and you will not cause worry to anyone. Good nutrition is very important for health. Stay away from outside foods. These could be contaminated. While eating, try to remain cool and calm as tension leads to stress and this leads to many illnesses. And then sleep is equally important for seven hours every night. Staying awake till late hours causes irritation and ill-health. Getting up early is very healthy. And the third suggestion is exercise and physical activity. So many people go for Yoga. You must try to learn these from someone who knows it or try other forms of physical exercises that will always keep you fit. Jogging is very good to stay fit and fine in body and mind. A good physical health is reflected in equally good mental health. You must stay away from filthy literature and people who tend to spoil the mental make-up of a person. Just remember, if character is lost, everything is lost! Indulge in creative activities. A good health is for life. This is a capital which will stand by you for all times. Do let me know how you are keeping up with your health.

Your elder brother
Anurag

Descriptive Letters

(Sample-3)
Writing a Letter to Chacha/Chachi Wanting to Spend Holidays with Them

Address:
Date:.......

Dear Chacha and Chachiji,

I trust you all are well. I wrote to you earlier that this Dussehra vacation, I want to spend with you. It has been quite some time I ate Panjiri made by Chachi. It would be kind of killing two birds with one stone. Sight-seeing and good food together. I may reach there by 14th of October. I have learnt that Bhubaneswar is a new city built over the old one. Besides spending two days is Bhubaneswar, I would like to visit Nandan Kanan also to see the tigers. A visit to the Buddha and the Jain caves and the Kalinga war remnants are also on the cards. Then we will visit to the magnificent Konark to see the Sun Temple. I would next proceed to Jagannath Puri to see the Jagannath Temple. Finally, I would also like to see the Dham, one of the four established by Shankaracharya. I look forward to spend a day on the Puri beach too. I have expressed my wish list, but I don"t know how many will actually fructify. Kindly fix a suitable time-slot as per your convenience. Convey my love to Alisha.

Your loving nephew,
Anubhav

(Sample-1)
Emotional Letters
Letter from a Pre-marriage Lover to his Beloved

Dear Deep

My life, my imagination beyond my dreams, Deep – I have become a kind of slave to you. In any direction, I look, I notice is you. Here there and everywhere. It appears you are mocking at my perplexity or wonderment. I just can"t describe the sense of fulfilment I get from these imaginary visuals. Here things have turned out a little worrisome as my so called sister, Astha has spread rumours (in fact, they are true) about our love for each other. My friend circle are pulling my leg. Every time, they drag me despite showing displeasure, I feel ecstatic. I am anxiously awaiting your mail. Take care!

Yours only
Anand

Delhi
Dated:........

(Reply)

Dear Anand

I received your letter. In fact, it was a poem in the shape of prose. I must be congratulated for transforming you into a poet. To tell you the truth, I have derived no pleasure by coming to Shimla from Delhi. Three days of wondering here without your company has sapped almost all the energy out of me. No enjoyment, no pleasure. Truly speaking, I have stopped going out. Shimla appears dry without you. Neither the mornings are pleasant nor are the evenings romantic. There is no youthful flurry either in the vegetations or in the mountains. The element of attraction is just not there in Shimla. Do you know why? It is just because of you are not here.

Yours always,
Deepshikha

Shimla
Dated:.......

(Sample-1)
Travel-Related Letter
My Haridwar Trip

Dear Sanjay,

India is a land of pilgrim centres. Slopes of mountains, rivers banks, ponds or sea-shores, you would find them everywhere. No wonder, foreigners describe India as a land of pilgrim centres. And Haridwar is one such popular centre.

Haridwar is situated on the banks of the River Ganges in the state of Uttarakhand. The Ganges flows down making way from the icy mountains of the Himalayas. The water is pure and icy cold. It is said that taking a dip in the river washes away the sins committed by us in the past. Though scientists discount this theory, nevertheless, they admit to acquiring enormous mental peace and tranquillity following a bath in the Ganges.

Despite Hardwar being is a small town, people from all parts of the country flock to this place. It is reckoned as a prominent city since times immemorial. A mela (fair) known as the 'Kumbh Mela" is organised every 12 years during which lakhs of people from every corner of the country visit to take a dip in the Holy River.

A number of temples are situated on the banks of the Ganges. There is a place called 'Har Ki Paudi", which is very popular among the pilgrims. This place was originally built on the bank of the Ganges, but now the river has changed its course and flows a little distance away from the site. However, a canal has been constructed at the 'Har Ki

Paudi" through which the river water still flows. A number of people gather at this spot every day. Temples of prehistoric times built to pay obeisance to Gangaji and Shivaji are worshipped since early morning till evening. After the sunset, people offer their prayers to Ganga *maiyya* and let off lit earthen lamps in the River Ganges. The scene presents a breathtaking view of the whole area. Thousands of pilgrims and visitors flock the place; to such an extent that literally no place is left to accommodate any more.

In the nearby hills are situated the temples of Mansa Devi and Chandi Devi. A ropeway exists to reach the Mansa Devi. We decided to make use of the aerial ropeway to visit the temple. It was a trip to remember. Our trolley stopped about 100 metres from the temple due to electrical problem. The moment was truly fearful. People began to panic. It was hard to comfort them. A peek down below was enough to send shivers down the spine. A quiet thought flowing river, series of hillocks and dense forests – all were contributing to the deadly heart-stopping moments. However, I that had the trolley not stopped, I wouldn"t have paid attention to nature"s posture. I mentally made a note and surmised that walking to the temple delivers a different kind of phenomenon altogether.

I admit to have made a number of pilgrimages, but I think I would never forget this heart-throbbing and eye-dropping experience of Haridwar.

I wish to visit this place with you in the coming season.

Yours affectionately,
Atul Saxena

Mixed Type of Letters

Letter writing is not a compartmentalised activity where you stay within a certain boundary. It depends upon who you are writing to. While business letters stay within defined parameters, personal letters, especially to close ones, overlap. While writing, some writers flow along and tend to mix up descriptive subjects with emotional or philosophical ones.

(Sample-1)

Letter to Wife

Dear Deepti,

I hadn"t been able to write to you for quite some time. Just work pressure and nothing else. However, this evening, I was feeling very lonely and hence, decided to go to India Gate. It"s very lovely to look at and quite impressive. Properly mowed lawns present an attractive scene. Fountains placed along and birds flocking along add to the serene beauty.

I came to visit this place but I just didn"t enjoy one bit. I always thought of telling you as and when I passed any attractive place or scene. But well, there was none to speak to. I, perforce, had to keep my mouth shut.

I was simply bored of not having you by my side. I wish you were there with me. Despite my best efforts, I couldn"t enjoy the visit.

Next time, when you are here, I will make sure we go together and enjoy the beauty of the place.

Rest all is fine!

Yours,
Sagar

Delhi
Dated: ....

(Sample-2)
A Letter to Husband

My Dearest,

I trust you are hale and hearty. We reached Banaras yesterday from Allahabad. We went to the Sarnath temple. The temple is very attractive to look at, but the statue of Bhagwan Buddha was beyond description. The paintings and images inscribed on the walls attract one from a distance. These paintings describe the prominent legacy of the life of Bhagwan Buddha.

The place is truly praiseworthy. You just won"t tire roaming around. The still existing remnants at the place reflect the relic of the glory of the bygone days.

Dear, it was a visit hardly worth remembering simply because of your absence. I couldn"t enjoy the boat ride either, the kind we had last year during our Banaras trip. How mesmerising was that boat ride – a one in a lifetime affair! Can one ever forget that?

Yours lovingly,
Ananya Angrish

Banaras
Dated:

(Sample-3)
Letter from a Student to a Teacher

Dear Sir,

The time I left Allahabad, I had hoped to travel throughout the country. But in the middle of my trip, I reached such an important place where I needed to stay for some time. It is Delhi. The place is situated on the bank of River Yamuna. I wish to understand the culture, its people and the surroundings. I am writing below whatsoever information I have been able to gather about the city. I hope you will apprise me with your ideas.

Delhi today is a huge metropolis. For all practical purposes, Delhi now is a conglomeration of a number of towns and cities. It reflects the architecture and beauty of an old city superimposed by a new one. It is a city where you would find people of different cultures thoughtprocesses, different ethos and religions and from different towns and cities. Everyone seems to be free to choose any vocation or profession. No restriction is imposed on anyone. Despite the city boasting of everything, there is no emotional attachment, and hardly any intimacy, closeness and co-existence. It is a highly individualistic, concrete jungle, literally no one to share your views, opinions and thoughts. Just work and very little scope for personal life.

This realisation about materialism confounded me no end. The government says the city is truly on way to bigger things in life. It has progressed much and is close to final destination. But what one observes is that there is tremendous disaffection among people, discontentment is on the rise, intolerance is touching new heights and there is distrust all through.

Sir, there is nothing that can"t be achieved under your guidance. I need your guidance to dispel the misgivings about this great city crossing my mind. Kindly enlighten me with your thoughts how to go about interpreting the values that Delhi professes and represents.

Yours obediently,
Jai Prakash

Okhla, Delhi
Dated:

Section – 4
Social and Public Letters

Social Correspondence

Social Correspondence

Letters that demand spreading of awareness to check and to put an end to prevalent issues adversely affecting the society are covered under the head, 'social correspondence". Intercaste marriages, marriage dissolutions, or female foeticides are some of the issues that immediately necessitate intervention and action. A few examples are given below:

(Sample-1)

Name and address of the sender
Dated:

Sri Devesh Choudhary
President, Zila Panchayat
Naharpur

Sub: About Intercaste Marriages

Dear Chaudharyji,

It has come to my notice that you are organizing a social meet in the coming month. We observe that the intercaste marriagess are gaining ground in the society quite rapidly. Therefore, please do not bring forward any resolution that condemns and punishes such marriages. I do agree that intercaste marriages sometimes let-in havoc in the lives of girls. Currently, the girls are not literate enough to easily take to such marriages on their own. It is mostly the boys who are taking the initiative. Therefore, to think about banning this kind of tying the nuptial knot will generate discord within the families.

It would be worthwhile creating educational opportunities for girls. The best course is to make them as qualified as boys. This would enable them to take a conscious decision in matters of selecting a suitable companion for themselves. There is no alternative to taking such a course of action.

I am writing this to apprise you with my views since I would be out of town; and am in no position to attend the meet.

Yours sincerely,
Gaurav Garg

(Sample-2)
Suggestion for Prevention of Divorce

Dear Radhika,

I have received your letter yesterday. I feel greatly perturbed that your relations with Rajiv have sunk to such an extent that you are considering the option of divorce. Are you left with no option? Is divorce the only choice left? Would you gain anything from dissolution? By the way, is there someone else in your life ready to tie the knot?

I still think Rajiv is a nice person. I may be wrong but I feel there is some kind of ego clash between you two. While I am not for woman always bending backwards to accommodate, nevertheless, I see no harm in trying to find a middle ground. Moreover, there is a child to be looked after, so please give compromise a go.

Look around, you will find our culture and societal norms provide stability to marriages. We ourselves have literally fought over many times; and shortly afterwards, came to our original selves. Disagreements between a husband and wife are a phenomenon that happens off and on and every time it occurs, the word, 'divorce" shouldn"t cross our minds.

I sincerely hope you will consider my views in the right spirit. Divorce is no solution; rather it creates more problems – both personal and social. If you are in a state of anger, think about it some other time. But give it a sincere and serious thought on this vital issue. You would find there is a valid reason to stay together.

Please write to me with a cool head.

Your friend,
Navneet Parihar

(Sample-3)
Suggestion to an Editor

Dear Arvind,

Your daily newspaper is coming under increasing influence of English words these days. Despite you being an editor, this rising tendency gives me jitters, an uncomfortable feeling. Hindi words – even the popular ones – are being replaced with English ones for no rhyme or reason. What was the great idea to substitute 'Vishvavidyalaya" with 'University"? There are many words whose substitution is just not required. I think, as an editor, it is your moral duty to diffuse this tendency, or nip this practice.

I am fully aware of the preference of the owners to run the newspaper purely in the manner they decide and if employment is to continue, editors have to succumb to their policies. This is not the correct perspective. You can, at least, offer your viewpoint. Newspapers carry a responsibility to march forward the cultural mores and also to reinforce cementing the social traditions.

More or less identical policy of 'encouraging English" is being sought to be implemented in our newspaper, but I have been successful in resisting thus far. If forced to decide one way or the other, don"t you think it would be a good idea to form an organisation and start a newspaper of our own? Do you have any idea, suggestion, etc?

Looking forward to your considered views on all these issues!

Yours sincerely,
Avinash
Sandhya Dainik

(Sample-4)
Social Invitation

Ms. Anita Aggarwal
Secretary, Stri Samaj
Kurla, Mumbai

Dear Sister,

I feel pleased that you have become secretary of the *Stri Samaj* of Kurla. Law and order situation in Mumbai has deteriorated to a great extent. I am calling a meeting of Mumbai, *Stri Samaj*. Time has come when women need to protect themselves. My wish is to have such women"s security bodies is every nook and corner. Major problem is that unsocial elements try to get friendly with women, pass vulgar and lewd remarks and otherwise become a nuisance to them. Incidence of rape is on the rise. Poor girls are lured into marriage only to be sold later on. Young girls are being trafficked. Government agencies are practically helpless before mafia indulging in such activities. Political leaders worry for nothing except remembering you at the time of elections. Women are the worst sufferer of this attitude. There is a meeting organised on 13th July, 2013. Please arrange to reach the *Stri Bhawan* at Dadar at 2:00 pm.

Yours sincerely,
Kamna Achrekar
Secretary
Brihad Stri Samaj, Mumbai

Letters of Complaint

No one is pleased complaining. When a person gets tired of seeking resolution to some issue and the concerned officials just don"t take notice, the complainant decides to take things forward to higher authorities to press for necessary grievance or removal or corrective action. Such letters are termed as *complaint letters*. Examples of complaints are, non-receipt of money orders, registered letters, telegrams, gas connection, non-servicing of telephones, theft, indecent behaviour of bus conductors, railway staff, etc. Failure of cleanliness of common areas, such as, garbage pile up, upkeep of roads, failure to maintain regular power supplies, water supplies, diverting supplies meant for public distribution into open markets, careless attitude of civic employees, etc., come under the same heading. Resorting to public complaints should be backed with solid evidences.

(Sample-1)

[Personal]

Non-delivery of Money Order

Name and address of the sender
Dated:

In charge, Post Office
Gopal Mandir Post Office
Chattri Chowk
Ujjain (M.P.)

Sub: Non-delivery of Money Order

Dear Sir,

I had sent from this post office a money order for ₹ 4,000/- addressed to my father at Bhawanipur.

This morning my father informed me that the said money order has not reached him till now.

My mother was to undergo an eye surgery at the Jiwan Nursing Home during the last month. Unfortunately, for want of money, the operation couldn"t be carried out. A number of visits to the post office there elicited no response from the staff saying that no such money order ever arrived.

Due to sheer indifference of the post office staff, my family had to suffer undue hardships. Will these people be able to visualise the difficulties imposed on them for no fault of theirs?

I request you to kindly look into the matter seriously and help deliver the money promptly. I have enclosed a copy of the money order receipt for your reference.

Thanking you,

Yours faithfully,
Anurag Sharma

(Sample-2)
Unbecoming Behaviour of the Bus Conductor

Name and address of the sender
Dated:

The Manager
Maharashtra State Road Transport Corporation
Thane

Sub: Unbecoming Conduct of the Bus Conductor

Dear Sir,

I wish to draw your kind attention to the unbecoming conduct of the Ramnagar Depot, bus conductor. Last 20th November, I travelled with my family from Narayanpur to Ramnagar Depot on bus no-M10 Q4572.

The fare from Narayanpur to Ramnagar is ₹ 10/- and therefore, for six persons it comes to ₹ 60/-. I gave him a ₹ 100/- note and expected the balance amount to be paid back. Saying that he would refund later when he gets it, the conductor moved forward to collect fares from other passengers. When we reached near our destination, I reminded him but to no avail. He evaded me under the pretext of not having the required change. We had to finally get down at Ramnagar without getting the due amount of ₹ 40/-

The badge number of the conductor is 6734.

I request you to take note of the above incident and initiate necessary action so that the said conductor refrains from acting likewise in future.

Thanking you,

Yours faithfully,
Kulvant Shinde

(Sample-3)
Non-functional Telephone

>Name and address of the sender
>Dated:

The Zonal Manager
MTNL
Kalatalab
Kalyan (Maharashtra)

Sub: Telephone No-23768549 – Not Working

Dear Sir,

I reside in Bhim Nagar locality within Kalyan Telecom Zone. For the past 15 days, my telephone no- 23768549 is practically dead. I had lodged a complaint on 15th of this month but to no avail. The token number is 347. When enquired a few days back, the fault was attributed to the underground cable wiring. Had it been so, the telephones of my neighbours wouldn"t have started functioning. They too were told about the fault in cable.

Clearly, the fault is not been attended to with any seriousness. My father is a heart patient. We may need the services of a telephone any moment.

I request you to depute your linemen at the earliest so that the telephone instrument is set right promptly.

Thanking you,

>Yours faithfully,
>Ajit Pawar

(Sample-4)
Irregularities in the Supply of Gas Cylinders

Name and address of the sender
Dated:

The Manager
Baldev Gas Agency
Bhav Nagar (Gujarat)

Sub: Irregularities in the Supply of Gas Cylinders

Dear Sir,

    The consumer number of my gas cylinder connection is 5674. Three weeks back, I had requisitioned your office for a refill cylinder. I regret to inform you that despite 20 days having elapsed, no refill is in sight. It is but common knowledge that your line staff ensures prompt delivery of refills to those willing to pay ₹ 20-25 to them by way of extraneous consideration. Others are doled out some innate and frivolous replies. An honest consumer has to wait at least 15 to 20 days before he gets supply. The hardship we have to suffer is untold. The attitude the linesmen bear is simply one of indifference.

    I request you to take note of the above, investigate the matter and issue strict instructions for timely and regular delivery of refills.

    Thanking you,

Yours faithfully,
Dilip Kulkarni

(Sample-5)
Complaint to Railway Authorities
Aronima Textiles

Address:
Date:......

The Chief Commercial Manager
Central Railway
Kalyan

Sir,

Yesterday we secured the delivery of four bundles of Banarasi saris sent by the Kamal Textiles, Varanasi wide goods receipt no.......... Date...........However, the packing of one of the bundles was found broken. The matter has been duly reported to the Assistant Station Master, Kalyan. As per the bill, each bundle contained 100 Banarasi saris. While the three bundles correctly had 100 saris as mentioned, the bundles with broken seals contained only 96 saris. The pilferage of 4 saris amount to a loss of ₹ 8000/- to us for railways are fully responsible. For your perusal, we are enclosing the bill as received by us. You will get to know the cost of each sari. We request you to conduct suitable enquiry and compensate us for the loss caused in this transaction.

Thanking you,

Yours faithfully,
Name

(Sample-6)
Complaint Regarding Damaged Product
Jagan Furniture

Address:
Date:

M/S Omega Furniture
20, Furniture Bazaar
Ulahas Nagar

Sir,

We are in receipt of the parcel sent by you on dated. On opening the parcel, we discovered that five showcases and three dressing case had their glasses broken or damaged. Further that seven showcases had glass coverings that don"t fit properly. It appears that the fault with the staff at the packing counter. We had shown the damaged showcases and dressing cases to the truck driver. Kindly send an expert to rectify the error; at the earliest.

Thanking you,

Yours faithfully,
Name

(Sample-7)
[Public]
Irregularities in Power Supply

Address:
Date:

The Executive Engineer
Maharashtra State Electricity Board
Shanti Chambers
Vashind – 421601

Sub: Irregularities in Electric Supply

Dear Sir,

    I regret to point out the extremely irregular power supply people of Vashind suffer. The Friday cut-outs regularly but for no apparent reason is a great menace to the locality, as a whole. The power goes off again in the evening and the residents, particularly the students and traders suffer enormously. It"s difficult to sit at home or remain peaceful in the absence of power. Since examinations are at hand, students are a worried lot. We are at a loss of thought and reason as to why the power situation has become so erratic? We request you to look into the matter urgently and set the power supply in houses in order so that the people of Vashind can live a comfortable life.

    Thanking you,

Yours faithfully,
Name

(Sample-8)
Complaint Against Inadequate Water Supply

Address :
Date :

The Commissioner
Ulhasnagar Mahanagar Palika
Ulhasnagar

Sub: Inadequate Water Supply

Sir,

With deep anguish, we, the residents of Gandhi Nagar wish to draw your attention to the huge water scarcity being faced by us for a long time. The speed with which Gandhi Nagar developed has been commendable, but the water supply arrangement didn"t keep pace with it. People suffer acute water problem. Water is supplied once a day for about half an hour and comes with enormous force. But affer that often water taps remain dry for two consecutive days. At times, this leads to quarrel among the residents. For lack of adequate availability of water, the people have to perforce, fetch water from other areas or from boring pumps, which are few and far between. We had hoped that the establishment of Mahanagar Palika will lead to substantial improvement in the living conditions but the situation remains as before. We sincerely hope you will take some concrete positive steps to improve the water supply conditions in Gandhi Nagar.

Thanking you,

Yours faithfully,
(Names & Signatures of
few respectable people)

Date:.........

(Sample-9)
Lethargy of Bank Staff

The Branch Manager
Oriental Bank of Commerce
197, Paschim Vihar
New Delhi – 110063

Sub: Lethargy of Banking Personnel

Sir,
    I wish to inform you that I am quite sick of the attitude of your staff. There are three counters for making payments but two of them almost always remain closed leading to long queues in the lone operating counter. Often employees instead of attending to customers go to their colleague"s desk and start gossiping. There is a board within the bank displaying the schedule of average time taken to perform certain functions, for example a cheque presented for encashment is scheduled to be paid within 20 minutes but in fact, it takes something around 30-40 minutes. Cheques of other banks take 4-5 days for clearing. We request you to kindly instruct your staff suitably so that customers don"t have to face harassment or inconvenience.

    Thanking you,

Yours faithfully,
Name & Address

Dated:............

(Sample-10)
Irregularities at Post Office

The Post Master
Dak Bhawan
Sundar Vihar
New Delhi

Sir

    We, the residents of Sundar Vihar, are facing a lot of difficulties and lack of facilities at the post office for days on end as the posted materials remain unavailable. If the envelope as the available then the postcards may not. In fact, one or the other is mostly out of stock. Enquiries are rudely replied to. Another problem is the postal boxes are not cleared regularly. A card deposited inside the postal box may remain inside for some days. Dak distribution leaves much to be desired timely and correct delivery to the addressee is not always there. We request you to take suitable steps to remove the grievances of the people living in that area.

    Thanking you,

Yours faithfully,
(Residents of Sundar Vihar with
Name, Address & Mobile Number)

Dated:.........

(Sample-11)
Complaint against Dirt, Filth and Garbage in the Colony

The Sanitation Officer
Uttam Nagar
New Delhi

Sub: Filthy Conditions in the Colony

Sir

We request to inform you that in the last few months the gutter drains and sewerage systems are not being cleared properly. For lack of effective cleaning, filth and other materials choke the pipes leading to overflow. Dirty water gets into the houses. Sweepers don"t care at all. This leads to flies, mosquitoes and other disease carrying insects flooding the area and its environment. Fumigation is not done regularly to check and control the growth of such disease causing flies and mosquitoes. If things like this goes on any longer, epidemics may erupt. It could also lead to loss of life as well. We request you to kindly pay urgent attention to our pleas to restore proper sanitation in the area.

Thanking you,

Yours faithfully,
(Residents of Uttam Nagar
With Address & Mobile Number)

Date:..........

(Sample-12)
Sale of Subsidised Kerosene Oil in the Market

The Rationing Officer
Circle Office
Madipur
Paschim Vihar
New Delhi

Sub: Unauthorised Sale of Kerosene Oil

Sir,

    We the residents of Madipur want to inform you that off and on sugar is made available at the ration shop but kerosene oil, never. The shopkeepers complain that kerosene oil has not been supplied and that as and when it comes, delivery would be made. Despite lodging complaint in the register maintained at the shop, no improvement took place. In collusion with unsocial elements, grains, sugar and kerosene oil are being sold in the open market. We request you to look into the matter on an urgent basis and take strict action against the concerned shopkeepers and other colluding elements of the society.

    Thanking you,

Yours sincerely,
Residents of Madipur
Name & Mobile Numbers

Date:..........

Letters to the Editor

Newspapers and Magazines have a unique place in the society. They reflect the social, economic and political happenings in the society, when writing a letter to the editor (drawing his attention to the improvement of the power situation, cleanliness, news regarding social happenings, etc.) You must mention your name, address and telephone number. If you don"t want your name to appear with the letter, make a request to the editor to this effect but he must have your details.

(Sample-1)
Requesting the Editor to Publish an Article

Address:
Date:

The Editor
Dainik Hindustan
New Delhi

Sir,

    I am sending you a poem, *Mera pyara basta* for your perusal with a request to publish the same under the *Bachpan* column in the forthcoming Sunday edition of your esteemed *Dainik Hindustan*. I would be highly obliged for this favour.

    Thanking you,

Yours sincerely,
Name & Signature

(Sample-2)
Annual Subscription

Address:
Date:

The Secretary
Sahitya Academy
Ravindra Bhawan, 35 Ferozshah Marg
New Delhi 110001

Dear Sir,

    I am sending you by Money Order (MO) a sum of ₹.........towards the annual subscription for *Samkaleen Bhartiya Sahitya*. Please start dispatching the magazine as soon as the remittance reaches you.

    Thanking you,

Yours sincerely,
Name & Address

(Sample-3)
News Regarding Fire

The Editor
Lokmat
Mumbai – 400021

Sir,

    I have attached a news item on fire in the locality for the favour of publication in your popular newspaper. Kindly do the needful and oblige.

    Thanking you,

Yours faithfully,
Name & Signature

Encl: The news item :

Fire Engulfed 50 Houses in the Slum Colony

Last night, a razing fire engulfed the slum colony of Shadipur in New Delhi in which five lives were lost and about 20 grievously injured. According to the fire brigade sources, 50 houses were completely burnt. The fire began around 12 in the midnight and could only be doused in the next one and a half hours. Loss of goods and properties in the fire is estimated to be around ₹ 3 lakhs.

The injured have been admitted to the Ram Manohar Hospital. An enquiry has been ordered to investigate the causes of fire.

(Sample-4)
Dead Body Found

Address:
Dated:

The Editor
Navbharat Times
7, Bahadur Shah Zafar Marg
New Delhi

Sir,

I have enclosed a news item, *Unidentified body found* for publication in your esteemed newspaper. Kindly publish it at the earliest.

Thanking you,

Yours faithfully,
(Name & Signature)

Encl: News item attached :

Unidentified Body Found

A dead body aged between 20 to 25 of a male was found nude in Gandhi Nagar park in East Delhi! The body bore infliction by a sharp weapon on the chest, neck, shoulder, etc. The police believes the removal of clothes from the body was done to hide the identity. The Gandhi Nagar Police was tipped off by an unknown caller informing them of the body. The police took charge of the body and sent it for post-mortem.

(Sample-5)

Truck – Jeep Collision

Address:
Date:

The Editor
Navbharat Times
7 Bahadur Shah Zafar Marg
New Delhi

Sir,

I have enclosed a news item, *Truck – jeep collision* for publication in your esteemed newspaper. Kindly publish the news at a prominent place.

Thanking you,

Yours faithfully,
Name & Signature

Encl: The news item

Truck – Jeep Collision: Two Dead, Four Injured

Last night, there was a head on collision between a truck and a jeep at Mahipalpur on the Gurgaon highway. The impact was so great that the jeep became a rumble of metallic pieces leaving two occupants dead and four injured. The injured were admitted to a government hospital in Mahipalpur. The jeep was on its way from Alwar to Kanpur. The jeep driver, Manohar died on the spot. The truck driver was allegedly under the influence of alcohol and he turned the truck towards Mahipalpur road without giving any signal.

(Sample-6)
A Suggestion Regarding Materials Published in Special Section of Newspapers

Address:
Date:

The Editor
Navbharat Times
Mumbai

Sir,

    I am a regular reader of your newspaper. Every week, I anxiously await the *Suruchi* magazine that comes with the newspaper on Sunday. As a matter of fact, *Suruchi* is a storehouse of information. Every article, more so the column named *Hastakshar* is well written. To make *Suruchi*, a little more popular, I have a suggestion if Amritvani and 'Crossword" are also included, *Suruchi* will become lot more better in fact, it would tend to become a full-fledged literary magazine. I hope you will give my suggestion a due consideration.

    Thanking you,

Yours faithfully,
Name & Signature

(Sample 7)
To Check Smoking

Address:
Date:

The Chief Editor
Jansatta
New Delhi

Sir,

    The *Jansatta* of 4th November carried a news item informing that a youth below 18 was fined for smoking in Singapore. I hope such a law should be there in India also. You would notice that boys below 18 smoke on the road with gay abandon. It has practically become a fashion. In fact, there is nothing healthy about it at all. It is one of the leading causes of Cancer, Tuberculosis, etc. What is necessary is to have a check on promotions that encourage its use! Mere displaying advertisements on cigarette packs carrying messages of Cancer is not enough. Cigarette sellers around the school and college premises should be moved out at least 500 metres away and if necessary, fined. To inculcate in younger generation a sense of belonging to the nation, 'No Smoking Day" should be celebrated on a fixed date throughout the country.

    Thanking you,

Yours faithfully,
Name & Signature

(Sample-8)
Request Not to Display Advertisements in the Middle of a Programme

Address:
Date:

The Editor
Yashobhumi
Mumbai – 400017

Sir,

    In recent terms, there is a noticeable increase in time being given for advertisements; especially in the middle of popular programmes and serials broadcasted over the TV. Things have come to such a pass that not just during religion based serials or cricket matches, advertisements are being placed during news also and repeated every now and then.

    My suggestion is that if they are to be displayed at all, then they should be slotted at the beginning or at the end of the serial. We hope you will give the suggestions their due.

    Thanking you,

Yours faithfully,
Name & Address

(Sample-9)
Misbehaviour of Driver/Conductor of a Bus

Address:
Date:

The Editor
Hindustan
New Delhi – 110001

Dear Sir,

Off and on, we hear of the unbecoming behaviour of bus conductors in public transport. Last week, I experienced this in Delhi"s bus no DL 1P 6483! No sooner the bus started from Sarai Kale Khan Interstate Bus Terminal to Faridabad, then a heated exchange of words took place between a lady passenger and the conductor. The conductor used filthy language. When other passengers objected, the conductor threatened to deboard the lady passenger. When objected again by most of the passengers, the bus had reached Badarpur. There both the driver and the conductor got down from the bus unmindful of the inconvenience caused to the passengers. More than an hour elapsed before the bus started moving again.

The passengers suffered in the sheltering heat for no fault of theirs. Through your newspaper, I want to draw the attention of the senior Delhi Transport Corporation officials to the lack of decency and etiquette among your line staff and give them suitable training that such untoward incidents do not occur in future and if necessary, punish the bad apples amongst them.

Yours faithfully,
Name & Signature

(Sample-10)
On Gambling in the Colonies

Address:
Date:

The Editor
Navbharat Times
7, Bahadur Shah Zafar Marg
New Delhi

Sir,

These days gambling has spread its wings in many colonies. There are secret cells where they are organised. New faces turn up quite often. During the last one month, it appears to have solidified its tentacles. The matter has been reported to the police but the effect is zero. It appears some policemen are in collusion with the gambling operators. Gambling has raised a new question of law and order and security. Frequently, quarrels and fighting breaks out among the gamblers.

This disturbs the peace of the area. We hope you will publish this so that the authorities take necessary action to bring security to the society while acting seriously upon the gambling operators.

Yours faithfully,
Name & Signature

(Sample-11)
Bad Elements, Ruffians in the Society

Address:
Date:

The Editor
Rajasthan Patrika Dainik
Jaipur

Sir,

I want to draw attention towards the rising graph of incidences, such as crime fights, etc. between anti-social elements within the society. Newspapers carry news of goondaism almost every day. The sense of fear has grown among the overage people. Daylight robberies, murder, shootout, looting, molestation, rape, etc. have become almost like a regular news items. Such news have started shaking the conscience of people.

The question is how to get rid of it. Government says police personnels are being deployed in great numbers to stop the rot. Unfortunate outcome is that lawlessness is increasing in direct proportion to the increase in numbers of police personnels. People have a feeling that the police is in hand and glove with the anti-social elements. That"s why they are acquitted when the matter goes to courts.

I wonder what exactly the police is expected to do. Security, protection maintaining peace has gone to dogs. Unfortunately, due to the callousness and indifference of a few police and officers, the entire police department is earning a bad name. We must also recognise that political and bureaucratic interference prevents people from doing their best. Unless this interference is stopped completely, peace won"t visit the society.

I hope you agree with this.

Yours faithfully,
Name & Signature

(Sample-12)
To Prevent Road Accidents

Address:
Date:

The Editor
Jansatta
Mumbai – 400021

Sir,

    Through your esteemed newspaper, I want to draw the kind attention of the concerned authorities in the government towards frequent accidents occurring between the Mahatma Gandhi Road and Badlapur Road. Five accidents have taken place on this stretch of road during the last two months. Hospitals, offices and schools lie connected to this important road link. Being a road leading to station this results in continuous flow of traffic vehicles which fly past at a high speed. Absence of footpath leads to great numbers being compelled to walk on the road. Hence, I have a few suggestions to avoid accidents :

- Shopkeepers shouldn"t be allowed to park their vehicles on the road and be asked to use proper parking areas.
- Cart vendors should be moved away. This in itself would create enough space for pedestrians.
- Speed breakers and zebra crossings should be constructed in front of the Saraswati Vidyalaya. The speed limit of 10 km should be imposed on vehicular traffic.
- Traffic signals should be erected near the station and those breaking rules should be acted upon promptly.
- To allow for unhindered flow during rush hours, the traffic police should be posted at the various sensitive points.
- Keeping in mind the increasing vehicular traffic on the Badlapur station area, a subway should be constructed to allow people to reach offices and homes on time.

    I appeal to the municipal and traffic authorities to apply the above suggestions in order to prevent further road accidents.

    Thanking you,

Yours faithfully,
Name & Signature

(Sample-13)
Adulteration at the Petrol Pump

Address:
Date:

The Editor
Veer Arjun
7, Bahadur Shah Zafar Marg
New Delhi

Dear Sir,

Through your esteemed newspaper, I want to draw the attention of the government towards the activities, such as adulteration at the petrol pump in the Madipur locality. Kindly publish this within the 'complaints column" of your newspaper.

There is a colossal adulteration of kerosene oil in petrol in the Madipur petrol pump which is sold to the public. Unhindered, this is being done by the owners in collusion with authorities from the sales department who get bribed heavily. It is alleged that this nefarious activities is being resorted to on exchange for substantial sums. These government authorities are sucking the hard earned money of gullible public. Moreover, adulterated petrol ends up damaging the engine of the vehicles. The cost of maintenance of the vehicles goup in proportion to the adulterated mix. For want of alternative avenues, people have to perforce depend on this particular petrol pump to refill their tanks.

Taking the above factors into consideration, it is requested that senior authorities should clamp down the dubious activities by taking stringent action on the erring staff.

Thanking you,

Yours faithfully,
Name

(Sample-14)
Dirt, Garbage and Lack of Cleanliness in the Locality

Address:
Date:

The Chief Editor
Navbharat Times
7, Bahadur Shah Zafar Marg
New Delhi

Sir,

Through the columns of your newspaper, I want to draw the kind attention of the civic authorities towards the lack of cleanliness in the Trans Yamuna localities. Roads and lanes of Gandhi Nagar have become such a casualty of lack of cleanliness that everywhere one can see garbage piled up. The area is in utter neglect now. It has become all the more after the elections got over. Filth and odour fill the locality so much so that the people find it difficult to live healthy. A number of meetings with higher ups brought force no improvement. Failure to take prompt action could result in epidemics spreading its wings. We request health department authorities to step up cleanliness on a war footing.

Thanking you,

Yours faithfully,
Name

(Sample-15)
Opinion on Rising Prices

Address:
Date:

The Editor
Manthan
Mumbai

Sir,

I am sending you an opinion price on the relentless price rise for publication in your esteemed newspaper with a view to draw the attention of the government to arrest the price rise. I hope you would spare adequate space in your newspaper.

Thanking you,

Yours faithfully,
Name

Encl: Opinion price

Relentless Price Rise

A *band* is organised every other day by one political party or another on the closure of factories and companies pushing the general public into unemployment, corruption and black marketing. This has led people to a situation worse than before. It has compelled people to wonder if they would comfortably earn enough to feed their family. The situation becomes worse if you have guests at home, whether its grains vegetables, oil or fruits, the prices have gone through the roof. If consider the plight of a family, where there is just one earning member and three depend including school going children. How would he make both ends meet? Will a middle class family able to survive. Politicians just talk about removing poverty and once in power do things that aggravate the price situation by raising the prices of essential commodities. How will people of this country be able to squarely meet the high prices?

(Sample-16)
Opinion : Today"s Indian Woman is Empowered

Address:
Date:

The Editor
Navbharat Times
Mumbai – 400001

Sir,

    I am sending you an opinion piece, 'Today"s Indian woman is empowered." I hope you will publish this within the 'people"s voice" column.

    Thanking you,

Yours faithfully,
Name

Encl: Opinion piece

Today"s Indian Woman is Empowered

In the Indian society, men and woman are complementary to each other. One doesn"t survive without the other. The Indian society is basically patriarchal. Women and children of the family take the name of the father. There are people who opinion that women don"t have the leadership qualities required to guide the family quietly forgetting that men themselves admit to incompleteness of family without women and that they are the backbone of the family. Today, women are educated, responsible and self-dependent.

They contribute to the family and society, be it being a daughter , sister, mother, statesmen, warriors, physicians, scientists, philosophers, kings and queens – all come out of the wombs God has bestowed woman with. They learn the first lessons of life, speaking, walking, learning, eating food, etc. all in the lap of a woman.

How else would you describe a quality other than as enlightened we all agree that mother, nature has ingrained women with enormous fortitude and patience. It is commonly said that behind every successful man, there is a woman. Now women are breaking all barriers and moving shoulder to shoulder with men folk in all spheres, such as, education, medicine, science, technical education, computer, politics, judiciary, literature, sports, nursing etc. of which primary education and nursing are considered their prerogative. After independence, there has been a phenomenal rise in the enlightenment of women. Mrs. Indira Gandhi led India as the Prime Minister for many years. Mrs. Vijaya Laxmi Pandit became the President of the United Nation"s General Assembly in 1953. Among leading politicians, Sucheta Kriplani, Sushma Swaraj, Sheila Dixit, etc. occupy prime places. Justice Leela Seth of the Delhi High Court became a luminary in her own right.

Who can forget the name of Kalpana Chawla? The first women paratroopers, Geeta Ghosh and aircraft commander Saudamini Deshmukh have glorified Indian women no end. The first woman IPS officer, Kiran Bedi continues to influence women in every field of life. Menfolk have come to accept women as partners in every walk of life.

Women of today have truly become emancipated and enlightened in all respects.

(Sample-17)

[Appeal]

Donation Sought for Treatment

Address:
Date:

The Editor
Yasho Bhumi
Mumbai – 400017

Sir,

    Kindly publish my appeal seeking donation for medical treatment in your esteemed newspaper.

    Thanking you,

Yours faithfully,
Name

Encl: Appeal

Donation for Treatment of Blood Cancer

The 30 year old Dinesh Kumar is a resident of Pant Nagar. He is a renowned sculptor and has been admitted to a hospital in the aftermath of the diagnosis of blood cancer. The doctors attending on him estimate an expense of ₹ 5 lakhs on account of chemotherapy and bone marrow transplantation. Two months back his father expired and there is no one else in the family to raise such a big amount.

    Serving humanity is the highest form of service. We appeal to all the citizens to contribute their might so that the precious life of Dinesh Kumar is saved. Benevolent people may kindly send a cheque or cash to the Cancer Patients Aid Association, Nav Jeevan Memorial Hospital, Samta Uddhyan Pant Nagar-2 (A\C Dinesh Kumar). We would be highly obliged for any kindness.

    Regards,

Name :

(Sample-18)
Appeal for a Kidney

Address:
Date:

The Editor
Jansatta
Mumbai

Sir,

    Kindly publish our humble appeal in your esteemed newspaper.

Thanking you,

Yours faithfully,
Name

Encl: Appeal

Appeal for Donating a Kidney

My father, Suryabhan is being treated at the Deen Dayal Upadhyay Hospital since last month. Doctors have declared both his Kidneys dysfunctional. In this respect, he urgently needs help. We would be grateful from the bottom of our hearts if some benevolent person comes forward and donates one of his kidneys that could save my father"s life. Kind-hearted donors may donate to the Nephrology Department, Deen Dayal Upadhyay Hospital, Delhi.

Correspondence with Insurance Companies

Trade and commerce has a close relationship with insurance firms. The insurance of companies protect them against loss, accidental damage, theft, etc. That"s why business houses consider it imperative to insure their assets from any unintended economic loss. Reasons to enter into correspondence with insurance companies may arise on account of the following:

1. Enquiry for insurance of life and property
2. Related to premium
3. Claim against damages

(Sample-1)
Making Enquiry
Ajay Pustak Bhandar

Phone Number
                                              18 Nai Sarak, New Delhi
                                              Date: 28 January, 20XX

The Manager
Oriental Insurance Company
Chandni Chowk,
Delhi

Sir,

   I am interested in insuring my shop. Kindly let me have various policies available on this account.

   Thanking you,

Yours faithfully,
Ajay Kumar
Proprietor

Correspondence with Post Offices

We enter into correspondence with post offices due to a variety of reasons. Sometimes, it becomes necessary to write to them seeking information about the arrival of an important document, non-receipt of a letter, change in address, complaints, resolution or for other commercial reasons. The writer of such letters should come to the point without unnecessary verbosity, while using a polite language.

Samples of correspondence with post offices :

(Sample-1)
Regarding a VPP Sent

Acharya Prakashan
23/1, Main Road, Gandhi Nagar
Delhi – 110031

Telephone:....... Delhi
Letter No:......... Dated:.......

The Superintendent of Post Office
11/9, Main Road, Gandhi Nagar
Delhi – 110031

Sir,

We had sent a VPP packet on the 4th of May, 2012 containing books worth ₹ 5,000/- to Pustak Sadan, Bareilly.

The party has informed that the VPP has not reached them till date. Kindly investigate the matter, and help in delivering the same to the addressee.

A photocopy of the postal receipt is enclosed for your necessary action.

Yours faithfully,
Vijay Acharya
Proprietor

(Sample-2)
Seeking a Post Box Number
Acharya Prakashan

Phone No:...... Address:
Ref No:.......... Date:.........

The Superintendent of Post Offices
Head Post Office
Krishna Nagar
Delhi

Sir,

    We want to be allotted a post box number for our official correspondence. Kindly let me know the detail about obtaining one.

    Thanking you,

Yours faithfully,
Vijay Acharya
Proprietor

(Sample-3)
Change of Address to the Post Office

Phone No: Address:
Ref. No. Dated:

The Post Master
Daryaganj
New Delhi

Sir,

    Recently, I have changed my residence and moved into a new house. This new house too falls within the jurisdiction of the Daryaganj Post Office. I have written my old and new address herewith. Henceforth, kindly ensure that all mails are forwarded to this new address.

Yours faithfully,
Surendra Kumar

(Old address)

(Sample-4)
Non-Delivery of Mails in Time

Phone No :   Address:
                                                                                                                              Date:

The Post Master
GPO
Jhansi

Sir,

    It pains me to write that despite many complaints in the past, letters and mails are still not being delivered in time. The new postman assigned for this area delivers mails here and there without caring to deliver at the correct addresses. Often letters are delivered so late that the significance of a letter is lost. I am an insurance agent and on account of late deliveries, I have suffered a loss of around a lakh in the last month only. If things don"t improve, I may have to take the matter to the consumer forum. It is my request to take action immediately to improve the timely deliveries of mails.

Yours faithfully,
Prakash Parmar

Section – 5
Job-Related Letters

Job-Related Letters

Job-Related Letters

Every organisation, whether government or non-government run aided by officials and staff, as such, every organisation has to arrange for the engagement of employees. It is done either through calling for applications from prospective, interested persons or on deputation or transfer within the organisation. Persons looking for employment either send in an application mentioning their qualifications or apply in response to vacancies advertised in the newspapers.

Types of Employment Letters

Correspondence with regard to employment begings right from notification of vacancies till the issuance of appointment letters.

- Notification of vacancies
- Communicated with media for publicity
- Receipt of applications
- Written tests/interviews
- Verifications of credentials of selected candidates
- Notification of selected candidates
- Issuance of appointment letters to selected candidates

Notification Regarding Vacancies

A notification is published once the vacancies and respective qualifications have been decided upon. This has to be done very carefully. The following points must be taken into consideration.

- Complete address of the organisation
- Complete details of the department of the issuer of the notification
- Details of vacancies, such as: number of vacancies, names of the posts and places of postings, etc.
- Details like formats of applications, etc. methods of sending applications, their last date and addresses, to which they are to be sent.
- Educational qualifications, experience, reservation, etc. also must be clearly indicated.

(Sample-1)
Wanted

Applications are invited by Career Commerce College Maharana Pratap Nagar, Bhopal for 5 posts of lecturers in commerce. Essential qualification is a first class post-graduate degree in commerce with age, minimum 21 years and the maximum should be 35. Interested candidates may sent their applications latest by the 20th of January, 20XX to Career Commerce College, 24 Maharana Pratap Nagar, Bhopal. Applications received after the last date will not be considered.

Dated
Principal
Career Commerce College
Bhopal

(Sample-2)
Wanted One Office Assistant

Wanted one honest and hard-working assistant for our Delhi Branch. Maximum age 40 years, knowledge of Hindi and English, typing and shorthand is a must, salary as per qualification. Apply with full particulars and send it to Post Box No. 7890, Nariman Point, Mumbai.

Correspondence with Media for the Release of Employment Notification

Government and private business houses use various media outlets, such as newspapers, magazines, radio, TV, etc to inform vacant positions. The first step towards this end which the organisations take recourse to is calling for advertisement tariff cards from the media keeping the importance of the target area and the financial strength of the company. The media selects where vacancies are to be advertised. Following are the samples of correspondence:

(Sample-1)

Jaico Motors
(Leading Distributors of Cars and Two-wheelers)

Telephone No:

34 Moti Nagar, New Delhi
Dated: February 18, 20XX

Ref No: 2012/Advt/135

The Advertisement Manager
Navbharat Times
7, Bahadur Shah Zafar Marg
New Delhi

Sub: Advertisement Tariff

Sir,

 From time to time, we release advertisements and other important circulars for publication in various newspapers. We request you to kindly send us a copy of your advertisement tariff for our consideration. We would appreciate if you include the tariff for special supplements also.

 Thanking you,

Yours faithfully,
Neeraj Saraswati
Manager

(Sample-2)
Arti Vastralaya
(Saree Manufacturer and Distributor)

Telephone No: Address:
                                                                                                                                                           Date:

Ref No:

The Director
Doordarshan Kendra
Vadodara (Gujarat)

Sub: Advertisement Tariff

Sir,

    We are interested in releasing advertisement of our colourful sarees on various regional channels as also on the National Channel No-1 of the Doordarshan. In this regard, kindly send us your latest advertisement tariff list to enable us to decide on the channels we wish to release advertisements.

    Thanking you,

Yours faithfully,
Dherendra Bhatia
Manager

Requested Letters/ Cover Letters

Request letters represent our identifications and credentials. They draw attention of the receiver to think about ourselves, give consideration to why a particular group of letters have been written, their purposes etc.

Request/Cover Letters and their types:
- Employment-related letters
- Admission-related
- Convenience-related
- Material-related
- Permission-related
- Issuance of certificates
- For proper and fair decisions

Employment-related

An application sent for seeking job is known as an application-related to employment. Such letters are written based on the information gathered through the newspapers. While writing an application to an employer, the source of information must be identified.

Salient Points while Writing an Application

- Application must be written on a plain white sheet
- Typed briefly and to the point
- Use one side of the paper only
- There should be margins on all four sides
- Complete address of the sender should be mentioned
- Abbreviations should not be used
- Should be free of grammatical errors
- Highlight the important milestones of your career
- Carbon copy must never be sent
- All documents asked for in the advertisements must be attached
- Qualifications and references should not be unduly highlighted
- If Postal Order/DD is to be attached, your name and address should be written on the back.
- If photo is also enclosed, it must bear the applicant"s name and address
- Original documents should not be enclosed
- If one is applying for a job, while being in employment, then please send the advance copy to the prospective employer and another copy through your current employer, if required.

(Sample-1)
Application for the Post of Salesman

The Rangarang Vastra Nirmata
45, Rajwada
Indore

Sub: Application for the Post of a Sales Executive

Dear Sir,

    I have reliably learnt that you are looking for a sales executive at your Bhopal branch to promote and sale 'Rangarang Sarees" manufactured by you. I have got 5 years of experience in this trade. I am offering my candidature for the above post. My particulars are as under:

Name	:	Nirbhay Singh
Address	:	House Address
Experience:	1.	Rajesh Vastralaya Indore as Sales Representative for Sarees from…….to………..
	2.	Rajkumar Silk Mills Surat as Sales Representative for Sarees from……………to………………

I hope you will give me an opportunity to prove my worth.

Thanking you,

Date:……..

                                                                                                   Yours faithfully,
                                                                                                    Nirbhay Singh

Encl:
1. Rajesh Vastralaya – Photocopy of experience certificate
2. Rajkumar Silk Mills – photocopy of commendation certificate

(Sample-2)
Application for the Post of an Accountant

The K. P. Publishers
26/2, Daryaganj
New Delhi

Sub–Application for the Post of an Accountant

Sir,

With reference to your advertisement in the *Dainik Samachar* dated 1st January, 20XX for the post of Accountants, I am sending my particulars and offering my candidature for the same.

Name	:	Gaurav Gupta
Father"s Name	:	Sh. Dheeraj Gupta
Address	:	120, Archana Apartment
		Paschim Vihar
		New Delhi-110063
Date of Birth	:	20th November, 1980
Educational Qualification	:	1. B.Com, Delhi University
		2. M.Com, Delhi University
Experience	:	Worked as an Accountant with Rahat Book Stall, Sarojini Nagar
		New Delhi from ……………….. to …………………

With regards to my qualifications and experience, I hope you will offer me a chance to prove my worth.

Thanking you,

Yours faithfully,
Gaurav Gupta

Date:………..

Encl: 1. Photocopies of Mark Sheets of B.Com & M.Com
        2. Photocopy of experience certificate from Rahat Book Stall

Written Examination/Interview – Notification

Application of candidates for different posts are checked and processed as per the eligibility criteria and those found suitable are asked to report for written exam and/or interview as the case may be. If the number of applicants is not large, direct interviews are conducted in normal course. Otherwise written exams of eligible candidates take place first and those found suitable are called for interview at a later date. Following are some of the examples of written and interview letters:

(Sample-1)

Anmol Vastra Bhandar
(Modern Clothing and Saree Manufacturer)
45, Chandni Chowk, Delhi

Telephone: E-mail:
Ref: Interview/2012/15

Subject – Interview

Dear Mr. Ravi Tiwari,

     With reference to your application dated………..for the post of Sales Representative (Saree) for our Moradabad branch, please report at the above address at 12 noon on dated……… You must carry the recommendatory letters from two respectable business houses.

     Thanking you,

Rupesh Kumar
Anmol Vastra Bhandar
Delhi

Job-Related Letters

(Sample-2)
Office of the Principal, Government College
Dewas (Madhya Pradesh)

Ref No: Interview/2012/134   Dewas, February 2, 20XX

Sri Akhilesh Tripathi
56 Sethi Nagar
Ujjain

Sub: Written Examination & Interview

With reference to your application dated……..for the post of Lecturer in English, please be informed that the written exam and interview has been scheduled as below. Please carry all your original certificates and a photocopy of each, while reporting here. No TA/DA is admissible to the candidates.

Lecturer (English) – written exam and interview

Written exam – 3rd March, 20XX, Time: 10 am to 12 noon
Interview – 3rd March, 20XX, Time: 2 pm onwards

Principal
Government College
Dewas

Verification of Credentials of the Selected Candidates

The documents submitted by the selected candidates are put through a verification process to ascertain their correctness and authenticity. Background checks are also made to establish that the candidates so selected are trustworthy. Correspondence with their previous employees are made to establish their efficiency, group behaviour productivity, etc. Some examples are given below:

(Sample-1)
Enquiry Regarding Credentials

Raghu Kitchen Bartan Bhandar
(Deals in Kitchen Utensils)

Telephone No: 20 Patni Bazaar, Ujjain

Date: April 2, 2012

Ref No:

Sri Ganesh Bhandar
Madhav Nagar
Indore

Sub: Regarding Sri Pradeep Sharma

Dear Sir,

    Mr. Pradeep Sharma has applied for the post of salesman. We have learnt from his application that he had worked in your shop sometime back. We would be glad to have your feedback regarding his reliability and trustworthiness. Please be assured that any information supplied by you would be kept private and confidential. We hope no inconvenience is caused to you in this regard.

Yours faithfully,
Raghuvansh Singh
For Raghu Kitchen Bartan Bhandar

(Sample-2)
Verification of Credentials

Shiksha Prakashan, Indore
Sadar Bazaar, Indore

Telephone No: 23, Sadar Bazaar, Indore
Ref No: 183   Date: May 5, 2012

M/S Rama Book Depot
Nai Sarak
Khandawa (M.P)

Dear Sir,

    Sri Sachin Verma has applied for the post of Accountant with us. He has mentioned your name in the reference column. We would be glad to receive your feedback regarding the suitability or otherwise of his candidature. We would appreciate an early reply.

    Thanking you,

Yours faithfully,
Viren Saxena
Shiksha Prakashan
Indore

Informing the Candidate of his Selection

After written examinations, interviews and background checks, the selection committee is convinced of the suitability of the candidate in all respects. Hence, the candidate is informed accordingly that he/she has been selected for the post. The candidate is then given an appointment letter. If this is not received by a particular date, he/she may directly report at the address mentioned below:

    (Address is mentioned here)

(Sample-1)
Saraswati Publishing House
Nai Sarak, Delhi

Telephone No: Delhi, Date: June 12, 20XX

Sri Satyanarayan Sharma
Daryaganj, Delhi

Dear Sir,

With reference to your application dated............., we are pleased to inform you that your name has been recommended for selection as a Branch Manager of our new branch at Kalyan, Mumbai. The appointment letter would be mailed to you by the end of this month.

Thanking you,

Suresh Sharma
Saraswati Publishing House
Delhi

Appointment Letter

An appointment letter is one that informs the selected person about his selection for a particular post at the designated office. Terms and conditions of appointment may also be indicated therein.

Contents of an Appointment Letter

- Address of the appointing office
- Name of the appointed person
- Designation of the person appointed
- Salary allowances and other perquisites
- Terms of appointment
- Date of appointment
- Duration of appointment
- Type of appointment – permanent, temporary or probation
- Date of joining
- Place of joining

(Sample-1)
Office of the Principal, Government College, Sagar (M.P)

Ref No: App/2012/16   Sagar, Date: June 23, 20XX

Appointment Letter

Sri Ajay Aggarwal is hereby appointed as an Assistant in this office. The salary payable is in the ₹ 10,000 – ₹ 15000/- grade. Please join your duty within 14 days from the date of issuance of this letter. You would be on probation for a period of one year.

Signature
Principal
Government College, Sagar

(Sample-2)
Arya Prakashan
55, Hawa Mahal Road, Jaipur

Telephone No: Jaipur, Date:
Ref: No:

Sri Akash Sharma
15, Naya Bazaar
Jaipur

Sir,

You are hereby appointed as a Sales Representative in our firm. You will be paid a consolidated salary of ₹ 10,000/- per month. Your employment would remain effective for one year from the date of your joining. Failure to join the duty before may entail cancellation of your appointment.

Signature
Aseem Rathi
Manager
Arya Prakashan

Section – 6
Business Letters

Business Letters

Writing a business letter is required in many different situations, from requesting or delivering information to place orders, coordinations, payment reminders to other business-related correspondences.

Writing a business letter is usually quite different from writing personal or other types of letters. Business writing needs to be crisp and succinct rather than creative; it stresses on specific subject matter and accuracy. It reflects the unique purpose and considerations involved when addressing a business context.

When writing a business or commercial letter, you must assume that your audience has limited time in which to read it; otherwise he is likely to skim over the correspondence. They want to know the gist or the 'bottom line": the point you are making about a situation and how they should respond.

Business writing varies from the conversational style to the more formal, legalistic style found in contracts. A style between these two is appropriate for the majority of mails and letters. Writing that is too formal and can alienate readers, and an attempt to be overly casual may come across as insincere or unprofessional. In business writing, as in all writing, you must know your audience.

In most cases, the business letter will be the first impression that you make on someone. Though business writing has become less formal over time, you should still take great care that the content is clear and that you have proof-read it carefully.

Business correspondence is written usually for the following:
- Communication media
- Written document
- Business expansion
- Creation of goodwill
- Proof
- Solution of problems
- Recovery of debts
- Advertisements

1. Communication Media
Business letters represent the views of the writer. Regular correspondence is necessary to maintain cordial relations with the customers and suppliers.

2. Written Document

Since it is difficult to remember the context of every correspondence, it is necessary to maintain a proper record of the same. Otherwise, there is a likelihood of missing a point or two.

3. Business Expansion

In order to expand business, it is pivotal to communicate with the existing as well as prospective clients. This is the only way to enter new markets.

4. Creation of Goodwill

Clear, crisp and to-the-point writing helps to establish and create goodwill of the organisation.

5. Proof

Business letter is a medium of communication between two parties. It serves as a written and recorded proof in case of any doubt or confusion between the parties.

6. Solution of Problems

Discrepancies with regard to supplies made is communicated to the other party through written correspondence with a view to resolve the issue. Verbal communication usually is not of much help.

7. Recovery of Debts

Where a customer has failed to pay dues in time, timely intervention by the way of reminders, business complaints or even taking to legal recourses are resorted to recover outstanding payments.

8. Advertisements

Direct mail is a form of advertisement. Sending direct mailers detailing the products is an important and economical means to propagate and communicate with the prospective clients.

Parts of a Business Letter

Heading (Sender"s Address)

In a business correspondence, the sender"s address (including firm"s name, telephone number, Fax number, e-mail ID, Trade Mark, etc) gererally are included in a letterhead. If you are not using a letterhead, include the sender"s address at the top of the letter followed by the date.

Number and Date

In a business letter, the serial number or the reference number and the date is mentioned below the company"s name.

The reference letter should be worked out in such a manner that by merely looking at the reference number, the correct file corresponding to that specific letter gets determined. Suppose the letter refers to an order during a financial year, 2011-12 and the letter number is 240, then the reference number of the letter should be read as Letter No: Order/11-2012/240.

This number should be followed by the date of the letter as was written, such as, January 10, 2011 or February 15, 2012, etc.

Internal Address

On the left side, just below the top, the recipient"s address is written, usually in three lines. In the first line, the name of the firm is written, in the second, street and the locality is written and then the name of the town/city and its PIN code.

Subject

Subject represents the central point of the correspondence. For example, Subject: Enquiry regarding rate

Reference

Where a letter refers to an earlier correspondence, the subject of that letter should be indicated to facilitate the recipient connected with this letter to the appropriate letter.

For example, Ref: Your letter no – Order/11-2012/250 dated 20th October, 2012

Address

The recipient should be respectfully addressed with a proper salutation. For example, Dear, My dear, etc.

Subject of the Letter

When writing a business letter, be careful to remember that brevity and conciseness are very important. Three important parts of the letter are: Initial introductory paragraph, main central part of correspondence and third, the action to be taken. In the first paragraph, consider a friendly opening and then a statement of the main point. The next paragraph should begin justifying the importance of the main point. In the next few paragraphs, continue justification with background information and supporting details. The closing paragraph should restate the purpose of the letter and, in some cases, request some type of action. Leave a blank line between each paragraph.

Complimentary Clause

The closing begins one line after the last body paragraph. Capitalise the first word only (for example: Thank you) and leave four lines between the closing and the sender"s name for a signature.

Enclosures

If you have enclosed any documents along with the letter, you indicate this simply by typing Enclosures one line below the closing. As an option, you may list the name of each document you are including in the envelope. For instance, if you have included many documents and need to ensure that the recipient is aware of each document, it may be a good idea to list the names.

Post Script

If you have suddenly remembered to mention something after the letter has been written, you may resort to the use of the option, 'Post Script".

Initials of a Typist

The person typing the letter should put his initials on the left bottom side of the letter.

Form of Business Letters

Title/Firm
Serial Number

Place
Date
Telephone:
Fax:
E-mail:

Address of the recipient

Subject:
Reference:

Dear Sir/Sir/Ma"m

Parts of a letter
a. Introductory part
b. Subject matter
c. Gist/action to be taken

Closing words
Signature
Name
Designation

Enclosure:
Typed by (Initials only):

Constituents of a Good Business Letter

1. Impressive
A recipient looks at the overall appearance of the letter. An attractive appearance leaves a good impression. This includes the quality of paper, ink, size of the paper, envelope, etc. If typed, it should be done neatly keeping clarity and brevity in mind. Envelopes should be respectfully addressed and adequately affixed with the correct postage stamp.

2. Clarity
The letter should be written in a simple language and the terminology must be easy to understand.

3. Completeness
The meaning of the letter should be clear to the reader at the first instance. If the idea is not written clearly, confusion may arise. This could also give rise to unnecessary correspondence.

4. Reality
The letter must contain facts, as furnishing of wrong information or imaginary observations should be avoided.

5. Courtesy
The letter should be courteous from energy angle. It should be polite and brief. A wrong and incorrect form of writing could harm the reputation of a firm or an individual. It should not be adulatory either.

6. Brevity
A letter should be brief and to the point and nothing should be written twice.

7. Ease
Only words that are in common parlance should be used. It must not smack of literary or scientific hypocrisy.

8. Convincing Effect
To be truly effective, the materials used should be of good quality.

9. Relativity
The letter must focus on one subject matter only. Topic not related to the letter should not be mentioned.

10. Flow
The letter should be written such that the content should appear to follow one after another in continuity.

11. Originality

The style of letter writing should be original and bookish language should be avoided.

Types of Commercial Letters

There are many kinds of commercial letters depending upon the circumstances. Following are the broad types:

- Regular commercial correspondence
- Irregular letters
- Enquiry letters
- Reply to enquiry letters
- Compliance letters
- Letters regarding dispatch of goods
- Supplementary letters
- Letters regarding agreements
- Complaint letters
- Letters regarding recovery
- Reply to creditors
- Personal business letters
- Sales letters

Regular Commercial Correspondence

It is a matter of courtesy that every business mail is replied the same day whenever possible. The letter should be written in such a way that the recipient gets the idea that his/her letter has been properly attended to. Given below are some of the examples:

(Sample-1)
Confirmation of Receipt of a Letter

Sri Ishwar Dayalji,
Barrister High Court,
Prayag
Sub:
Ref:
Dear Barrister Saheb

    Thank you for your letter which we received on................We will be able to take a decision on your manuscript on the Hindu law only after reviewing it. We request you to send us a copy of the same. Our coordinator is out of town at the moment. Once back, he will take up the issue of publishing it. Meanwhile, kindly treat this letter as the confirmation of your mail.

    Thanking you,

Yours faithfully,
Sandeep Jha (Manager)
(Name & Address of the Organisation)

(Sample-2)

Sri Ramnarayanji,
21 Gandhi Park Road,
Kanpur
Sub:
Ref:
Dear brother Ramnarayanji,

We have received your letter dated.................wherein you requested for information regarding toys manufactured by us in our factory. We have attached details regarding the type of toys we produce.

    We look forward to receive your esteemed order soon.

Yours faithfully,
Sri Prasad
Proprietor
Yashoda Toy Making Factory

(Sample-3)

Sri Indra Kishore
119 Nai Sarak
Delhi
Sub:
Ref:

Dear Sir,

    Received your letter dated………The amount of discount we have offered to you on our product is based upon our beneficial mutual relationship with each other. It is likely that due to the Government"s policies, some price fall is likely around the month of December. If you can hold back your fresh orders till then, the advantage of lower prices would automatically be passed down to you. We hope you will keep this in mind, while placing your next order.

Yours faithfully,
Vishnu Prakash
Vikram Cloth Mills

(Sample-4)

Sri Atma Sharanji
11, Sadar Bazaar
Kanpur
Sub:
Ref:

Dear Sir,

    We have received your order dated………for the purchase of vests for 100 dozen. Please recall our terms of business wherein we had mutually agreed for a 15% discount on a single order of 200 dozen vests. However, this time we have decided to offer you the stipulated discount on this order of 100 dozen vests only. We hope that our supplies will give you no reason to complain. In future, we will offer you the terms ordinarily reserved for our most valued customers. If you happen to visit Delhi, please be our guest instead of staying in a hotel. You would feel pretty homely at our guest house.

Yours faithfully,
Nand Kishore
Delhi Baniyan Store

(Sample-5)

Prof. Vimal Kirti Rathore
Banaras Hindu University
Varanasi
Sub:
Ref:

Respected Prof. Vimal Kirtiji,

    We have received your manuscript on………. You are desirous of having 10,000 copies of the printed book. You have not mentioned the type and quality of paper on which it is to be printed. Within a week, you would receive a few samples of the paper we could use. Whatever quality of paper you select, 10,000 copies of the book would be printed within the next 15 days.

    Thanking you,

Yours faithfully,
Bhawani Singh
Delhi Printing Press

Letters of Acknowledgement

Letters of acknowledgement are written when the decision-makers or authorised, designated persons are absent from the office or when the type of enquiry can"t be replied back soon. The letter is just to acknowledge that the letter in question has been received, lest the writer may wonder if it has actually been received by the addressee.

(Sample-1)

Sri Vipin Bihariji
Secretary District Council
Meerut
Sub:
Ref:

Dear Sir,

We have received your letter dated………..We are unable to attend to your query at the moment. Reason being that the director"s office is shifted to Mussorrie during summer. We have accordingly forwarded your letter to that office, who will in due course respond to your mail.

   Thanking you,

Yours faithfully,
Manager
Omega Printing Press

(Sample-2)

Sri Vishwarajji
56 Strand Road
Kolkata
Sub:
Ref:

Dear Sir,

   We have received your letter dated………There is an acute shortage of product in the market for which you have placed your order. There is a heavy fluctuation in the prices of most of the products since the last one week. Though we have sent a few orders, the market is experiencing a heavy turmoil in prices. As regards to the confirmed prices, we will only be able to communicate next week. We regret the delay in fulfilling your order.

Yours faithfully,
Manager
Special Order Suppliers

(Sample-3)

Sri Gajrajji
20, Tehsil Road
Meerut
Sub:
Ref:

Dear Sir,

    We have received your mail dated………..We are sorry to inform you that books ordered by you may not be supplied this week. As a matter of fact, the book is in the press and for some unforeseen reason, it is getting delayed. We wonder if we could do as requested in your letter. Only last week, our director has given orders to a reputed agency to supply books to one of the booksellers in Meerut.

    If the terms of the agency have been agreed to, then we may consider sending you supplies by around 10th of the next month under the terms and conditions set out for the bookseller in question.

    Thanking you,

Yours faithfully,
Manager
Ramkrishna Prakashan

(Sample-4)

Sri Hansrajji
Prop: Raj Shoe Store
Varanasi
Sub:
Ref:

Dear Sir,

    We have received the samples sent by you and have put them for evaluation by our chief technician. It could take some time since he is ill for the last five days. He will check the estimation and quality of the samples before any decision is taken. We hope to manufacture as per the sample and let you know its pricing by next week. We hope this little delay won"t cause you any inconvenience.

    Thanking you,

Yours faithfully,
Manager

For Zaidi Shoe Factory

(Sample-5)

Sri Harshvardhanji
Civil Lines
Bareilly
Sub:
Ref:

Dear Sir,

    Thank you for your order dated…………..We are extremely sorry that we are not in a position at the moment to inform you if we would succeed in sending two dozen, big-size carpets this month or not. We have placed the order for intermediate materials, three months back. But for one reason or another, the same is not yet ready for dispatch. In the face of uncertainty of materials, kindly confirm how much time you are prepared to grant us to execute the order.

    Thanking you,

Yours faithfully,
Hemprakash Ahuja
Prop. Great Carpet Stores

Letters of Confirmation

In business, often two parties discuss some issues and take an informal decision. This form of letters put the conversation in writing for record.

(Sample-1)

Sri Narayanji
Civil Lines
Allahabad
Sub:
Ref:

Dear Sir,

    This morning your representative visited our office to discuss important business terms with our director. We are ready to sell our product in Allahabad through you and agree to the discount structure as discussed in the meeting mentioned above.

    Thanking you for your cooperation,

Yours faithfully,
Manager
Shyam and Sons

(Sample-2)

Sri Shashibhushanji,
Bhushan Shoe Merchant,
Station Road,
Ghaziabad
Sub:
Ref:

Dear Sir,

    We are pleased to learn from your representative that you have a large shoe shop at Chowk Bazaar in Ghaziabad. You would be pleased to know that we supply our products throughout India. We have discussed at length the terms and conditions governing the agency with your representative.

    Please confirm by mail if the terms are agreeable to you. Should any clarification is needed, please don"t hesitate to put that down while replying.

    Thanking you,

Yours faithfully,
Manager
Royal Shoe Company

(Sample-3)

Sri Deepak Marwah,
Marwah Studio, Noida
Sub:
Ref:

Dear Sir,

We are interested in shooting a film in your studio. The discussion our representative had with you has been vetted by our directors.

Since the discussion held in your office was face to face and not in writing, we are putting across the vetted decision of our board for your kind approval.

Kindly send the duplicate copy of the agreement so that the shooting begins immediately.

Thanking you,

Yours faithfully,
Managing Director
Sagar Films Pvt. Ltd.

(Sample-4)

Sri Vaibhav Vyasji,
Radio Manufacturers,
Chandni Chowk, Delhi
Sub:
Ref:

Dear Sir,

One of your representatives visited us this morning. He discussed the issue of acquiring our agency in Bareilly for selling radio sets manufactured by you.

We agree to the terms and conditions for picking up the agency. We further agree to deposit the security money as agreed between us.

Following are the points of agreement. (Enumerate the points here under)

Kindly acknowledge validating the agreement. If any clarification is needed, please state that by return of the mail.

An early reply is solicited.
Thanking you,

Yours faithfully,
Bareilly Radio Stores

(Sample-5)

Sri Shambhu Nathji,
Raja Ka Talab,
Varanasi
Sub:
Ref:

Dear Sir,

As discussed this morning on phone, we express our agreement to the terms and conditions of doing business with you. We believe both of us would be immensely benefitted by our working in the long run.

We are sending you a copy of the draft agreement. Please go through it and satisfy yourself that every point is clear. However, if any remains, please write to us immediately.

Kindly send your approval at the earliest.

Thanking you,

Yours faithfully,
Manager
Sona & Rupa Pvt. Ltd.

Enquiry Letters

Letters seeking enquiry/information about any product should be written briefly and to-the-point. Otherwise, it leaves a bad impression about our firm.

These letters should be easy to read and understand. No scope for confusion should be left.

Following are some of the examples:

(Sample-1)

Sri Nandan Nagendraji,
Publisher and Bookseller,
Daryaganj, Delhi
Sub:
Ref:

Dear Sir,

    Sometime back, we got an opportunity to glance at the front-cover of one of the books published by your publishing house. It was excellent. The illustrator seemed to inject life into the cover.

    May we request you to give us the name and address of the illustrator? Since we are not a business competitor, we are sure, you would be forthcoming with the information sought and not question the sanctity of our request.

    Kindly inform us the name and address of the illustrator at the earliest.

    Thank you.

Yours faithfully,
Manager,
J.D.N.Company

(Sample-2)

Agra Khilona Company
186, Sadar Bazaar, Agra
Sub:
Ref:

Dear Sir,

    We are interested to purchase 500 velvet-made teddy bears within a week. We understand, no other company comes close to your craft, finish and styling as far as manufacturing teddy bear is concerned. Kindly inform us on phone. My telephone number is 22167467, whether it may be possible to supply 500 numbers of teddy bears within a week.

    We hope to have your confirmation at the earliest.

    Thanking you,

Yours faithfully,
Manager,
Ashok Toys Company

(Sample-3)

Manager,
Hamdard Dawakhana,
Lal Kuan,
Delhi
Sub:

Dear Sir,

Your dawakhana is popular not just in Delhi, but all over India. May we have the price details regarding your top products such as, Sharbat Rooh Afza, Sharbat Badam, Sharbat Sandal and Sharbat Khas.

Kindly inform us the prices of the desired products by the return of the mail. We look forward to place our order soon.

Thanking you,

Yours faithfully,
Manager,
Gorakhpur Sharbat House

(Sample-4)

Tyagi & Tyagi Sports House
Chandni Chowk,
Delhi
Sub:

Dear Sir,

It gives us pleasure to know that sports equipments used in the sport of hockey, football, tennis, cricket and volleyball are available with you at quite a reasonable price; and that you maintain quite a large stock of them to choose from.

Would it be possible for you to send one of your representatives along with the samples and best prices? What is the commission available for sellers of these equipments?

We would be grateful to you for sending a representative at an early date.

Thanking you,

Yours faithfully,
Sports Secretary
Modi Higher Secondary School

(Sample-5)

Manager,
Usha Sewing Machine Agents,
Nai Sarak,
Delhi
Sub:

Dear Sir,

    The Usha machine that we bought last year is performing well in all aspects. We look forward to buying another 10 machines. Have you brought out any improved version of this model? If so, kindly brief us of the benefits and advantages of using this machine.

    Thanking you,

Yours faithfully,
Manager,
Anuj

Reply to Enquiry Letters

Every letter enquiring about your product or services must be replied promptly, accurately and clearly. The appropriateness of replies invite attention, and increases the chances of orders. A bland reply is a recipe for no business. Hence, it is important to be careful while attending to such an important source of business development.

    A few samples are given below:

(Sample-1)

Manager,
J.D.N. Company,
Jaipur
Sub:
Ref:

Dear Sir,

We are in receipt of your letter. We are thankful to you for appreciating books published by us. As desired by you, we are giving below the details of the illustrator who shaped the design of the front cover:

Sri Mukund Saxena

House No- 5754, Gandhi Nagar, Delhi – 110031

Mobile No – 9832653477

Do let us know if we could be of some additional use for you.

Thanking you,

Yours faithfully,
Nandan Nagendra
Director, Publisher and Bookseller

(Sample-2)

Sri Sanjivji,
Manager,
Ashok Toys Company
New Delhi
Sub:

Dear Sir,

We are thankful for your letter seeking our likelihood to supply 5oo teddy bears.

We wish to inform you that we will execute the order one week after receiving the full amount. The price of 500 teddy bears is ₹ 50,000/-. Since your order is quite substantial, we would be pleased to offer you a discount of 40%.

Kindly confirm your order at the earliest.

Thanking you,

Yours faithfully,
Navin Parihar
Proprietor
Agra Khilona Company

(Sample-3)

Sri Amogh Pandey,
Manager,
Gorakhpur Sharbat House,
Gorakhpur
Sub:

Dear Sir,

    We are pleased to learn that you are desirous of purchasing our *sharbats* in sufficiently a large quantity. We are enclosing a price list for your reference.

    We hope to receive your order at the earliest.

    Thanking you,

Yours faithfully,
Manager,
Hamdard Dawakhana

(Sample-4)

Sports Secretary
Modi Higher Secondary School
Modi Nagar
Sub:
Ref:

Dear Sir,

    We are delighted to learn that you are fully aware of the huge stock of sports goods that we maintain at our end.

    We would like to inform you that one of our representatives will meet you next Monday along with the samples and price list.

    Please have a close look at the samples; and place your order at the earliest.

    Thanking you,

Yours faithfully,
Manager,
Tyagi & Tyagi Sports House

(Sample-5)

Manager,
Anuj Messrs,
Station Road
Gonda
Sub:
Ref:

Dear Sir,

We feel pleased to learn that the Usha sewing machine manufactured by us is serving you with utmost satisfaction.

That you wish to order another 10 machines symbolises a great amount of trust in our product.

We hope to receive your order at the earliest.

Thanking you,

Yours faithfully,
Manager
Usha Sewing Machine

Stop-gap Letters

This kind of letter is written during the absence of the minister or when the owner or director of a firm is out of station. It is also written when the head of the organisation is busy with other pressing engagements. These letters are a kind of *acknowledgement* letters.

A few samples are given below:

(Sample-1)

Sri Vinod Pawarji,
129, Queens Road
New Delhi

Dear Sir,

Our director regrets that he will not be in a position to reply to your letter this week due to prior engagement elsewhere. The director"s meeting is being held almost daily due to which he is not getting time to attend to ordinary work schedule.

He would respond as soon as he is free.

Regards,

Yours sincerely,
J.P. Nigam
Acting Incharge – Sri S.Khaitan

(Sample-2)

Sri Vishwanathji,
50, Strand Road,
Kolkata

Dear Sir,

This is to inform you that Sethji has gone on a tour to visit some agencies of the firm. It is quite likely that your letter may not receive due attention in the next 15 days. He is likely to be back by the 20th of this month. He would respond immediately upon his arrival here.

We sincerely regret the inconvenience caused to you.

Regards,

Yours sincerely,
P.S. Mishra
Acting Incharge – Sri Ramnath

(Sample-3)

Sri Ranvir Singhji,
11, Civil Lines
New Delhi

Dear Sir,

You had sought an appointment with our proprietor on Friday, 6th December at 5.00 pm. The proprietor regrets his inability to meet you at that time due to prior engagement. However, he would be glad to meet you at 5.00 pm on the following Monday.

We hope the above time suits you.

Thanking you,

Yours sincerely,
R.S. Gandhi
Proprietor
Acting Incharge – Sri Damodar Aggarwal

(Sample-4)

Sri Anoop Ganguly
234, Bara Bazaar
Kolkata

Dear Sir,

We received your letter today. We are sorry to inform you that Sethji is indisposed and is under medical care for the last three days. He has been advised complete rest. In the circumstances, we are not forwarding your letter for his attention. We hope you would forgive us for the unexpected delay.

Thanking you,

Yours sincerely,
Subhash Verma
Acting Incharge–Seth Damodar Prasad

(Sample-5)

Sri Ramsharanji,
Civil Lines
Bareilly

Dear Sir,

    We have received your letter just now. The proprietor is out of station and, therefore, it is not possible to give a proper reply to your mail this week.

    As soon as he attends the office next week, your mail would be placed before him on priority basis. We regret the delay.

    Thanking you,

Yours faithfully,
J.K. Kataria
Acting Incharge – Sri Badri Prasadji

Letters Regarding Products

Writing a letter for ordering a product or enquiring about a product are two different things. If you are only making enquiries regarding a product, please make a mention that only upon satisfaction with the price, design, etc the order would be placed.

Letters of this kind should furnish the following information:

- Article
- Catalogue Number
- Size
- Colour
- Model
- Other Specifications
- Unit Price
- Discount
- Total Price
- Destination
- Means of Shipment
- Terms
- Purchase Number
- Date
- Signature

A few samples are given below:

(Sample-1)

The Amul Dairy
Main Road
Ghaziabad

Dear Sir,

    Our hotel, 'Aabodaana" is quite popular in Delhi. We consume about 50kg of butter daily. Is it possible for you to fulfil this demand on a regular basis? If so, we would like to check the sample of butter and the price at the earliest.

    Thanking you,

Yours faithfully,
Manager
Hotel Aabodaana

(Sample-2)

Kishori Lal & Sons
Patel Nagar
New Delhi

Dear Sir,

    We had the pleasure of sampling your products that arrived in our office this morning. The samples looked attractive but the price appeared to be on the higher side. If you could offer us a discount of 15%, we may order 2000 pieces of each of the items.

    Please confirm your acceptability or otherwise of our proposal.

    Thanking you,

Yours faithfully,
Manager
Mohan Messra
Hapur

Letters Regarding Products

(Sample-3)

M/S Vimal Vastralaya
Naya Bazaar
Bhopal

Dear Sir,

We are pleased to inform you that we have in stock a huge assemblage of modern clothing in our warehouse. These are available on substantial discounted prices for the wholesale dealers.

We are running a stock clearance sale from 1st of February to the 15th February, 20XX. For every purchase in units of ₹ 10,000- entitles one to a coupon. A draw would be held on 15th February and the lucky winner would drive home a Maruti Alto.

We hope you would take advantage of this exciting offer!

Thanking you,

Yours faithfully,
Sunil Jain
Proprietor
Adhunik Vastra Bhandar, Indore

(Sample-4)

Mukesh & Sons
Rajdhani Marg
Jabalpur

Dear Sir,

We have hereby enclosed a price list of office equipments. We hope our attractive price structure would encourage you to place the order for the above.

Thanking you,

Yours faithfully,
Manager
Sanjay Office Equipments

(Sample-5)

The Saraswati Press
Varanasi

Dear Sir,

    We have received your letter and the catalogue yesterday.

    We have passed it on to our librarian. As per our library requirements, he will tick the required selections on the same catalogue and send back to us. We will forward the same to you for the execution of the order. You would receive it within this week.

    We are grateful to you for the warm cooperation.

    Thanking you,

Yours faithfully,
Suresh Singh
Principal
Agra College

(Sample-6)

Gangaram & Co
Chandni Chowk
Delhi

Dear Sir,

    Kindly send us samples and the price list of the biscuits manufactured by your firm. We will take a considered decision and hope to place a good order after assessing the samples (and the prices) sent by you.

    Thanking you,

Yours faithfully,
Manager
Leelaram Biscuit Stores

(Sample-7)

The National Toy Co
Sadar Bazaar
Delhi

Dear Sir,

You would be pleased to know that ours is the largest among all toy shops in Shimla. From the coming month, the tourist season begins and the sale of toys increases. We, therefore would like to replenish our stock this month only.

Kindly send us a copy of the catalogue along with the samples at the earliest.

Thanking you,

Yours faithfully,
Manager
Shimla Toys Stores

(Sample-8)

The Manager
Hotel Aabodaana
Fatehpuri Chowk
Delhi

Dear Sir,

We received your letter dated…..on …..

We feel pleased to know that the butter manufactured by us attracted your attention. As a matter of fact, this butter has achieved a class of success within two months what other dairies have not been able to do in years.

We look forward to receive your continued patronage.

Thanking you,

Yours faithfully,
Manager
Amul Dairy

(Sample-9)

The Principal
Agra College
Agra

Dear Sir,

    We received your letter dated…………….on………………. We are grateful to you for inviting us while placing orders for the supply of library books. We look forward to your esteemed order. We hope to get one very shortly. We will supply you the books as per your order.

    Thanking you,

Yours faithfully,
Manager
Saraswati Press

(Sample-10)

Hiralal & Co.
Chandni Chowk
Delhi

Dear Sir,

    We have received your mail dated………………..this morning in our shop. We are pleased to learn that you will be able to sell such a huge number of our products in the market. This year we have manufactured blankets in 20 different varieties and they are better in quality and design compared to the last year"s. We hope you would be pleased with the products and place your order in large numbers.

    Thanking you,

Yours faithfully,
Manager
Jeevan Ram & Co.

Logistics Loading and Transportation

Letter written regarding dispatch and transportation contain the following three elements:

1. Class of product
2. Date of dispatch
3. Manner of loading

With this letter in hand, the consignee can visit the transport company to ascertain the facts about the dispatch and in case of delay seek their help in locating the materials in transit. If there is no information forthcoming, the consignee can write to the consigner with regard to seek his/her assistance with regard to the arrival of the transported materials at his/her end. Such letters are called *tracers*.

(Sample-1)

Rama Publishers
45/4 Daryaganj
New Delhi

Dear Sir,

We are in receipt of your letter dated……………You have informed us that our order was dispatched on …………………..We regret to inform you that there is no confirmation regarding this, nor the goods receipt has been received by us. The transporter is unable to furnish us any details regarding the location of our order. Kindly look into it and inform us with the status of the order.

Thanking you,

Yours faithfully,
Manager
Premier Book Company

(Reply)

The Premier Book Company
Ardali Bazaar
Varanasi

Dear Sir,

    We feel sorry that the books have not reached you till date. We have checked with the dispatch department who have confirmed that books were loaded and transported on……………..We have sent a tracer to our rail road company and hope by tomorrow, we should have a definite information. Please be assured that in case we are unable to trace the parcel by next week, we will dispatch an identical set of books so that you don"t suffer for no fault of yours. We sincerely regret the inconvenience.

    Thanking you,

Yours faithfully,
Manager
Rama Publishers

Supplementary Letters

If happens sometimes that while writing a letter, or placing an order, we forget to mention one or other important points. To make up for some omission/s, we write another letter in which we mention all that was inadvertently missed out in the first letter. Such letters are known as *supplementary letters*. A few samples are given below:

(Sample-1)

Indo Trading Co
Chawri Bazaar
Delhi

Dear Sir,

We hope you must have received our mail dated………..wherein we had sought details regarding the availability of printing press related parts and prices (list was enclosed). While replying, please inform us whether you have a new Victoria Machine in your stock. What"s its price? The machine must be new and of the latest model. We look forward to receive your mail by the return of post. Upon receipt, we would be able to place an order.

Thanking you,

Yours faithfully,
Manager
J.D. Printing Press

(Sample-2)

Rakesh Book Depot
Haridwar

Dear Sir,

Last week, we had sent you the price lest of our books. We are enclosing herewith details regarding the published books that came out in the last week. We look forward to receiving your order from both the price tests. We hope you will be able to sell our books in good numbers at Haridwar.

Thanking you,

Yours faithfully,
Manager
Rama Book Company

Correspondence Regarding Agreement

An 'Agreement" between two parties is the backbone of business, a few samples of this nature of correspondence entered into is given below:

(Sample-1)

The Hamdard Dawakhana
Lal Kuan
Delhi

Dear Sir,

    You are well aware that we have a high regard for your products. Only worry on our part is that the prices appear to be on the higher side. A local supplier in Haridwar is prepared to supply at nearly half the price as yours. We would be saving on handling charges as well. We would be pleased if you consider offering us a competitive price so that we would be able to place regular orders. Looking forward to your mail at the earliest!

    Thanking you,

Yours faithfully,
Salman Siddique

(Reply)

Mr. Salman Siddique
Haridwar

Dear Sir,

    We received your mail dated…………..on……………….We feel pleased to know that you value our products. We do agree with your contention that our prices appear to be on a higher side, but it is mainly due to the fact that are invariably expensive. We would like to assure you that wherein our medicines start acting within a minute, products of other manufacturers may take a few days to elicit response. That"s not the real purpose of any medicine. We look forward to receiving your order at the earliest.

    Thanking you,

Yours faithfully,
Manager (Hamdard Dawakhana)

Letters Regarding Products

(Sample-2)

The Manager
The General Leather Shoe Factory
Kanpur

Dear Sir,

You would be pleased to know that we have opened a large store on the main road in Chandni Chowk, Delhi. We intend to place our order for shoes to be stocked in this shop. So far, we have procured shoes from 4-5 prestigious companies! We would be pleased to have a copy of your latest price list along with your most competitive terms and conditions for business. We would appreciate if you could depute your representative along with the samples. It would facilitate our ordering. If the samples and actual supplies match, we could be in for a long-run relationship. Please let us know your schedule at the earliest.

Thanking you,

Yours faithfully,
For Swadeshi Shoe Store

(Reply)

Swadeshi Shoe Store
Chandni Chowk
Delhi

Dear Sir,

We are in receipt of your letter dated................What you have heard about our quality is absolutely correct. There is no element of exaggeration in it. Should there be any difference between the sample shown to you and the product dispatched for sale we would forgo our price on that. Our representative will start from Kanpur on Monday evening and would reach you sometime in the afternoon, next day. He is carrying samples of a variety of shoes. You may place your order on this basis.

Thanking you,

Yours faithfully,
Manager (The General Leather Shoe Company)

Letters of Complaints

Complaint letters are written with a view to seek redressal against any grievance. These letters should be addressed in a very polite way.

Given below are a few examples.

(Sample-1)

John & Johns Co.
100, Strand Road
Kolkata

Dear Sir,

    We regret to point out that your deliveries always reach later than the expected date mentioned by you. Quite often, late deliveries lead to cancellation of orders, we had confirmed to dispatch by a certain date. We are made to suffer consequential loss of business and reputation on account of your delays. If this remains and the situation doesn"t improve, we would be forced to cancel all the current and future orders.

    We hope you will suitably appraise your dispatch and logistics section to improve timeliness to prevent rupture in our long established business relationship.

    Thanking you,

Yours faithfully,
Sandeep Tyagi

(Reply)

Sri Sandeepji,
New Product Company
Naya Bazaar, Delhi

Dear Sir,

We are in receipt of your letter dated….., this morning. We feel sorry for the inconvenience caused to you due to our late delivery. We would like to inform you that suitable instructions have been passed to the concerned department to oversee that such lapse don"t occur in the future.

We are sending you a price list and the necessary details of the products we have recently imported. Please be assured that we will take all necessary steps to prevent any damage upsetting our relations in future.

Thanking you,

Yours faithfully,
Manager
John & Johns Company

(Sample-2)

The Manager
Sri Baba Glass Works
Chandni Chowk, Delhi

Dear Sir,

We are in receipt of our order placed on you. It has been delivered through mail. Upon opening the packet, we were shocked to find the fragile glass materials in broken condition. In fact, more than falf of the goods were in broken and damaged condition.

No attention, it appears, was paid to the packing of the fragile materials with safe packaging. Furthermore, the product was found to be short-supplied when tallied with the invoice.

For lack of proper attention and care from your staff, we have incurred a huge loss. We hope, keeping our cordial relations in mind, you would investigate the matter and keep us informed of how this happened.

Thanking you,

Yours faithfully,
Manager
Haridwar Pottery Stores

(Reply)

The Manager
Haridwar Pottery Stores
Haridwar

Dear sir,

We are in receipt of your letter. We regret the error of addressing the parcel wrongly. In fact, the error occurred due to one of our loading staff.

However, to make up for the delay and damage, we are sending you another order parcel. We sincerely hope you will excuse us this time for our improper handling of the dispatch.

We assure you that such errors will not be allowed to happen anytime in future.

Thanking you,

Yours faithfully,
Manager
Baba Glass Works

(Sample-3)

The Proprietor
New Stationery Manufacturing Co.
Chawri Bazaar, Delhi

Dear Sir,

We have been having a very cordial relationship with your firm for the last many years. Keeping this in mind, we buy most of our stationery requirements from your Allahabad Branch. Of late, we have noticed that your new branch manager in not favourably inclined towards our firm. We have almost never received a sympathetic consideration to any of our queries/complaints. We wonder if he is trying to rupture relations between us. During the last one year, neither we properly received our orders, nor the book of accounts were reconciled to our satisfaction.

Kindly do let us know of your plan to take any remedial measure.

Awaiting an early reply.

Yours faithfully,
Kumar Sagar
Proprietor, Sagar Stationery Merchant

(Reply)

Sri Kumar Sagarji,
Stationery Merchant
Hindu Vishwavidyalaya Road
Varanasi

Dear Sir,

Your letter dated...... was received in our office on.............

We feel sorry to tear of the inconvenience caused to you due to the poor behaviour of our branch manager at our Prayag office.

We have received complaints of identical nature against the said branch manager. This unbecoming conduct has given us a bad name and loss of reputation in the market. In a meeting held last week, the directors have decided to call him back to the central office and someone more down-to-earth be seated to replace him.

We hope to remain the best parties in business and that we will always remember the benefit of your continued patronage.

Thanking you,

Yours faithfully,
Proprietor
The New Stationery
Manufacturing Co.

On Doing Business on Credit

Two factors deserve careful attention when a new business firm seeks to do business on credit.

1. Does the firm has financial standing to pay off the dues?
2. Will they pay off the dues?

These factors have to be duly ascertained and cross-checked. There are few who have the capability to liquidate the outstanding hurdle but are of doubtful character and babble to default. There are other types of faring also who work to pay off, but for one or other reasons are unable to do so. These factors should be carefully verified from one or the other.

Following are some of the examples:

(Sample-1)

Sri Banarsi Das
Civil Lines
Prayag

Dear Sir,

We are in receipt of your order dated..........

We checked our books of account holders but failed to find your name.

We are forwarding you a copy of credit opening form. Please fill the form so that we could take the next step towards dispatching your order.

We looks forward to establish a strong relationship with your firm.

Yours faithfully,
Proprietor, Gulzarilal & Sons

(Reply)

Gulzarilal and Sons
Chawri Bazaar
Delhi

Dear Sir,

Your letter dated............was received by us on..............

We feel pleased to learn that you are prepared to consider our request for enlisting us for extending your products on credit. We have filled up the credit opening form and also have enclosed herewith for your dispensation.

Though we are new to each other, but we are sure, our relationship will nurture rapidly resulting in mutual growth.

Kindly arrange to dispatch our order at the earliest. Customers are pressing us hard for deliveries.

Thanking you,

Yours faithfully,
Proprietor
Sri. Banarsi Das

(Samle-2)

Tyagi Bros. & Co.
Chandni Chowk
Delhi

Dear Sir,

    This morning we have received your letter dated............... along with the order. We feel pleased to consider sending our goods on credit. Kindly let us know the details of credit account you are holding with the other firms.

    Please expedite sending the details so that we are able to process your request at the earliest.

    Thanking you,

Yours faithfully,
Nanak Cand
Nanak Chand & Sons

(Reply to the above)

Sri Nanak Chandji
Nanak Chand & Sons
Strand Road
Kolkata

Dear Sir,

    We are thankful to you for your kind letter dated............

    As desired, we are giving the following names of the parties with whom we are maintaining credit accounts.

1. Messrs. Prayag Das & Sons, 45, Strand Road, Kolkata.
2. Messrs Mangalal & Sons, 107, Bara Bazaar, Kolkata.

    We feel pleased to inform you that the person who advised us to write to you was your son-in-law, Sri Randhir Bhist. We met in Mumbai.

    While the paper work remains under process, please don"t hold back the consignments. Otherwise, we may suffer loss of a big order for want of samples. We intend to use a few products of yours as samples. Kindly send the same at the earliest.

    Thanking you,

Yours faithfully,
For Tyagi Brothers & Co.
Proprietor

Letters for Debt Collection (Credit Control)

Many firms have a policy to clear off the outstanding of parties within a fixed period. But then time and circumstances subdue the momentum of regular timely payments. In such a situation. It becomes necessary for the supplier to send a polite reminder.

These are a few examples:

(Sample-1)

Rama Publishing House
Daryaganj,
New Delhi

Dear Sir,

While going through the book of accounts for the month of January, we discovered that an amount of Rs. 5000/-still due form you.

We work to finalise the account for January. Which to held up due to this receivable. Kindly expedite, sending this amount of Rs. 5000/- at the earliest.

Thanking you!

Yours faithfully,
Bal Mukund Sharma

(Sample-2)

Kumar Electronics
Chandni Chowk
Delhi

Dear Sir,

Perhaps your attention has not been drawn towards a small amount of Rs. 2067/- which remains outstanding in our account books since January.

May we request you to remit this amount by cheque at the earliest.

Thanking you!

Yours faithfully,
Manager
For Rajan Electronics House

Letters Regarding Products

(Sample-3)

Sri Ramanathji,
Ramanath Bartan Store
Patel Nagar
New Delhi

Dear Sir,

We want to bring to your kind notice that an amount of ₹ 1500/- is still outstanding against our supplies made in December. It is quite likely a case of 'overlook". Kindly arrange to send a cheque of ₹ 1500/- as soon as possible. For the past few months, there has been a slow-down in our receivables.

Kindly expedite.

Thanking you,

Yours faithfully,
Manager
Chetan Bartan Company

(Sample-4)

Sri Dhaniramji
General Merchant
Railway Road
Jhansi

Dear Sir,

As per our book of accounts for the previous month, a sum of ₹ 10,000/- is due to us from your side. Please make it convenient to remit the amount by cheque at the earliest.

We are due to release payments to our suppliers.

Thanking you,

Yours sincerely,
Manager
Arvind General Stores

(Sample-5)

Ramanuj Book Company
Khan Market
New Delhi

Dear Sir,

The payment for our invoice no…….. dated January 11, 20XX, for a sum of ₹ 4500/- is due from your side. This amount should have reached by the 1st of February, 20XX in the normal course.

Kindly expedite remitting the amount.

Thanking you!

Yours faithfully,
Manager
Atul Book Company

Replies of Debtors

It is observed that firms fail to live up to their commitments to clear dues for one reason or another. In the normal course, the firms schedule their payments based on receivables to their account. It they get delayed in getting their dues, the chain of scheduled dispersals is broken.

Since most of the firms face such crises one time or another, they are quite susceptible to accept pleas of another firm seeking extension of time. They are generally on the same page as far as delayed payments and their cascading effects are concerned. No firm likes to be reminded of their dues to another firm. They take a polite note and courteously agree for extension.

Given below are samples of such letters.

(Sample-1)

Sri Deen Dayalji,
Station Road
Moradabad

Dear Sir,

    We are sorry to inform you that we could not clear off your dues by the 3rd of June, the date of the scheduled payment. During the whole of last month, we remained busy with the new management. As such, dues of most of the parties were cleared.

    Beginning the week, we have begun dispatching cheques to the concerned parties. Your cheque will also be dispatched at your end this week.

    Thanking you,

Yours faithfully,
Gulzari Lal

(Sample-2)

The Punjab Toy Factory
Sadar Bazaar
Delhi

Dear Sir,

    We are in receipt of your letter dated...............

    We had sent you at least five letters seeking to set right the to commission payable to us, but not for once you chose to acknowledge or reply.

    We request you to amend your demand letter based or the commission agreed between us. As soon as such a mail arrives, your dues would be sent by cheque without delay.

    Thanking you,

Yours faithfully,
Manager
Haridwar Toy Merchant

(Sample-3)

Delhi Shoe Company
Karol Bagh
New Delhi

Dear Sir,

    We are in receipt of your letter dated……….. in which you have sought a period of 15 days to clear off our dues. We are glad to know that your bill of ₹ 5000/- due from the Municipal Committee has been cleared at your end, next week.

    We are sure you won"t take more than two weeks for our dues to be liquidated.

    Thanking you,

Yours faithfully,
Dheerendra Prasad

(Sample-4)

Bareilly Cloth House
Parivahan Road
Bareilly

Dear Sir,

    We are in receipt of your mail. We feel sorry to hear that the 'bountiful season" has not yet begun and this must have tied your hands in sending us the payment due to us.

    Though payment was not a priority, yet the arrival of a shipment has forced us to ask for funds. Without unduly subjecting you to pressure, we would be glad if you could make a part of the payment to prevent us from landing in an embarrassing situation.

    Thanking you,

Yours faithfully,
Manager
Raju Cloth House

(Sample-5)

Chandausi Toy Merchant
Station Road
Chandausi

Dear Sir,

We are in receipt of your letter dated………..We are sorry to say that despite five reminders from your side, we could not properly attend to them. Even since Bhai Sahab left for London, two months back, the working schedule has got somewhat disrupted. However, a fresh invoice in brief has sent to you incorporating the correct discount as agreed between us.

Kindly send the cheque for the due amount at the earliest.

Thanking you,

Yours faithfully,
Dorman Barbi House

Demi-Official Letters

Demi-official letters are written to those with whom you have become a little more friendly. Such letters are indicators of growing intimacy between two persons; and not necessarily a business relationship.

To the content possible, these should reflect closeness.

Greetings

Dear Anujji,

Kindly accept our warm wishes on the occasion of Deepawali. We hope our business relationship will attain new heights in the coming year.

Yours sincerely,
Sanjiv Katiyal

(Reply)

Dear Sanjeevji,

Thank you for your warm wishes. We too work and hope to see the new year turning a new leaf of prosperity in friendship and respect between us.

Yours faithfully,
Anuj

I have always treated you more like a friend, not like a business companion. On this occasion of Deepawali, I wish you the best in health and prosperity.

Yours faithfully,
Sheel Kumar Sagar

(Reply)

Dear Sheel Kumarji,

It gives me a lot of pleasure to sense your feelings for me more like a friend, not a businessman. I share the same feelings for you.

Please let me know when do you plan to visit us.

Your friend,
Vinod

Dear Bhuvaneshwarji,

I can"t put in words the sense of fulfilment I felt following our commercial engagement that began last year. I am sending you a calendar of the new year, as well as my best wishes. I hope the new year will bring you prosperity and a fruitful relationship between us.

Yours,
Dinesh Mohan

(Reply)

Dear Dinesh Mohanji,

Thanks for sending an attractive and colourful calendar. I reciprocate your warm wishes for the new year.

Like you, I also trust that our relationship will grow to enormous heights.

Yours ,
Bhuvaneshwar

Congratulatory Messages

Always remember to greet your business colleagues whenever they achieve some outstanding success. Such letters aid in improving relationships.

❋ ❋ ❋

Dear Akash Bhaiyya,

It is a matter of extreme pleasure for us to learn that your name has been promoted as a general manager. I am sure, your company would greatly benefit by recognising your talents.

Yours,
Bhuwan

❋ ❋ ❋

Dear Raj Kumarji,

You deserve a sincere congratulation on transforming your new printing press into a profitable venture. Very honestly, it was just not difficult for a person of your calibre.

Yours,
Anil

❋ ❋ ❋

Dear Sunilji,

Please accept my warm wishes on the occasion of your promotion as a manager. I felt mighty happy to learn this.

Yours,
Sudhir

❋ ❋ ❋

Dear Shiv Narayanji

I congratulate you on your success at manifesting on blade for threshing machine. No one has till now succeeded in making one so far.

I knew one day you would succeed. And you actually did!

Yours,
Harsh

❋ ❋ ❋

Dear Aseem,

I gathered from the manager that your firm has earned a profit of ₹ 5 lakh in just one year. This is the result of your hard work and dedication.

On this achievement, I congratulate you and your entire staff.

Yours,
Tribhuwan

Letters of Sympathy

Dear Sunil Mohanji,

I learnt with great dismay that a fire broke out in your Daryaganj godown and it engulfed goods of considerable value.

You have all my sympathies on this account. Please let me know if I could be of some use in this regard.

Yours,
Vaibhav

❋ ❋ ❋

Dear Anilji,

Just now I received the news of the sad demise of your wife. How can God be so cruel? I wholeheartedly share your bereavement in such an irreparable loss.

Yours,
Rakesh

❋ ❋ ❋

Dear Hardayalji,

I am pained to hear of your hospitalisation. By chance, the hospital is located close to our residence. Hence, we will certainly visit from time to time to check on your health and recovery.

As long as you stay in the hospital, your salary will be sent to your wife.

We are with you, always.

Yours,
Pravesh Rana

❋ ❋ ❋

Sales Letters

Almost all business correspondence has one objective–How to push sales? Therefore, a polished way of writing sales letters acquires great importance. It should be brief, to-the-point and written in an attractive way so that it impresses the addressee to consider purchasing the produced.

Some of the examples are given below:

(Sample-1)

Nityanandji,
Nitya Stationery Mart
Aligarh

Dear Sir,

    We are sending you a few samples of our calendars. We are quite sure, you would like them. Besides these, we have printed other calendars as well. If you like the samples, please don"t wait another moment to place your order. For expediting this, we would offer you a 40% discount.

    We look forward to receiving your order at the earliest.

    Thanking you,

Yours faithfully,
Manager
Ram Lakhan Calendar Co.

(Sample-2)

Sri Ram Singh
365/1
Burari, Delhi

Dear Sir,

    I was in Burari area last evening. I came across your house that is truly in a dilapidated condition. The roof appears very weak that could give way anytime causing injuries. I wanted to speak to you on this yesterday itself, but lack of time prevented me from doing this.

    I can check and inform you of the areas of repairs to avoid any untoward incident.

    Please take notice of my observation. If you desire, I would give you an estimate of the expenditure on repairs.

    Thanking you,

Yours sincerely,
Jayant Juneja

(Sample-3)

Devasheeshji,
519, GH-14
Pashchim Vihar
New Delhi

Dear Sir,

    We have located a house exactly as desired by you. Two bedrooms, one drawing cum dining hall, bathroom and balcony.

    This is an attractively built new dwelling unit with large windows (with glass panes). There is a part in the front where you can spend your leisure time.

    We hope the house matches your taste.

    Looking forward to meet you soon…….!

Yours faithfully,
Krish Associates
Proprietor

(Sample-4)

Sri Narayan Duttji
107, Narayan
New Delhi

Dear Sir,

    As we all know, life is all about action in motion. Full of activities. If not, one would not be able to be progressive. When you get tired with activities, you seek solace. What better way can there be other than sitting on a comfortable sofa?

    We are writing this to showcase our well designed and appropriately crafted sofa. Besides being a show piece in the drawing room, these sofas help you unwind in no time. The price is very affordable.

    We look forward to be of service to you.

    Thanking you,

Yours faithfully,
Manager
Tanishk Sofa House

(Sample-5)

Bhuwan Artist
9, Patel Estate
Kalba Devi, Mumbai

Dear Sir,

After having a look at your art works, we felt it necessary to inform you that art related products are arriving from Holland soon. The colours are fast and garnished to last a very long time. Alongside, new kind of brushes are also coming along to create sensitive painting works.

We are sure, you will visit our studio and place orders as per your need.

Thanking you,

Yours faithfully,
Kamal Art Shop
Proprietor

(Sample-6)

Smt. Ushaji,
Principal
Indraprastha College
New Delhi

Dear Sir,

We have made a plan to gift our reputed customers a set of valuable publications during this coming Deepawali. Attractive discount will apply to all those who subscribe to our popular monthly, *Sulabh Sahitya Mala* by remitting its annual subscription.

We hope you will make use of the offer and communicate the same to your friends, well-wishers and students.

Thanking you,

Yours faithfully,
Narendra Pustak Kendra
Manager

(Sample-7)

The Librarian
Hindu Library
Sadar Road
Kanpur

Dear Sir,

    You must have subscribed to a number of magazines and journals. We are sending you a copy of a magazine that we have started publishing since the last three months. Within this period, it has been greatly in demand and reputation. You must have heard that the 'Kalpna" magazine published from Hyderabad had described this magazine as a revolution in the publishing world and suggested readers to go in for regular reading.

    We are sure library users will appreciate you for your optimistic and forward-looking ideas.

    Thanking you,

Yours faithfully,
Kamaldeep 'Kanwal"
Publisher
'Kamla" Monthly

Section – 7
Government Communications and Letters

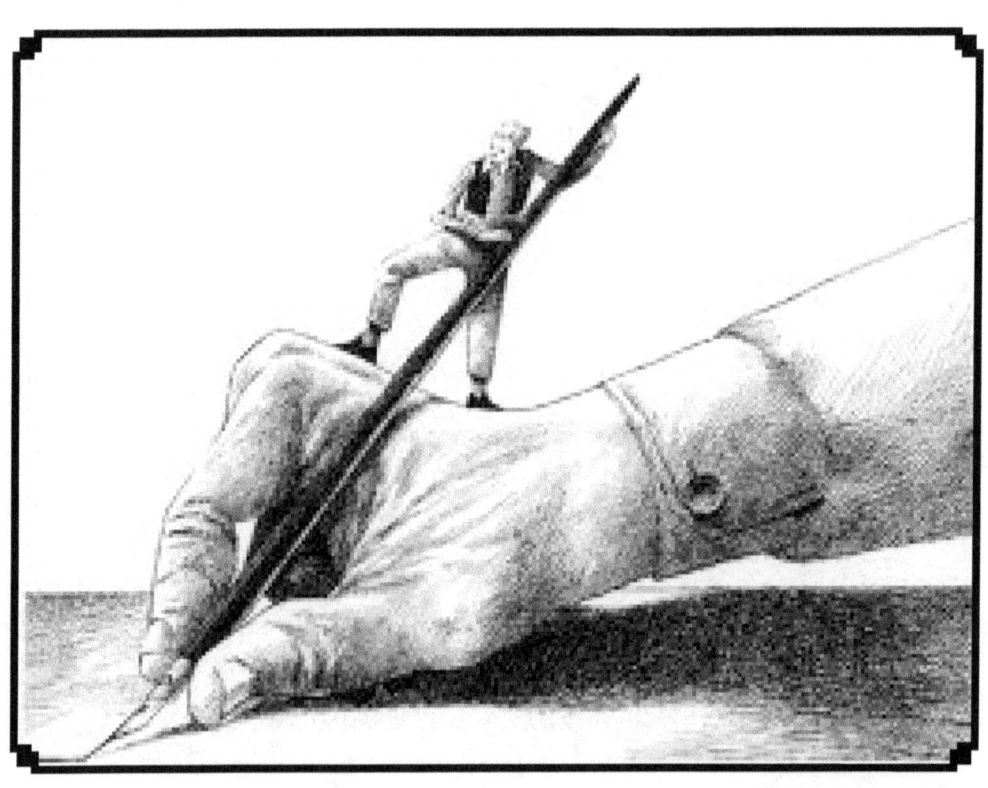

Government Communications and Letters

Government Correspondence

Government letters are those that are written by public servants/officials to someone for government-related matter.

Significance of Government Letters

The administration makes use of this form of communication to inform the general public on matters of importance, such as order, information or other important announcements. Following are the salient parts:

- ❑ All governmental orders are issued through letters.
- ❑ Appointments, promotions, demotions, retirement, extension of service, etc. are all communicated through letters.
- ❑ Authorisation and responsibilities besides duties are assigned through letters.
- ❑ The central government and the state government communicate with one another through official letters.
- ❑ Governments regulate their functions among various departments through letters.
- ❑ Governments direct and supervise functioning of educational institution, public sector undertakings and other statutory bodies through letters.

Parts of Government Communications

Letter No.

Letters are always numbered such that the departments, and other relevant sub-departments", files become apparent.

Name and designation of the sender

Name designation, department, etc. of the addressee.

Name of the sender department

On the left side letter number, while on the right side, the name of the sending department of the letter, place and date are mentioned.

Subject matter of the letter
Below the letter number, the place of dispatch and date, subject matter of the letter, etc. are written.

Reference
If this letter is with reference to any previous correspondence, that number is also mentioned.

Salutation
Quite often, salutation is not mentioned in official letters.

Subject
The subject matter of the letter is broadly divided among three parts:
1. Introduction part
2. Explanatory part
3. Conclusion-Action required to be taken

Signature and designation of the sender
On the right side and below the conclusion, signature of the person signing the letter and his designation is written.

Enclosures
If something (papers, etc.) is enclosed with the letter, it should be mentioned here.

Copy
If copy/copies of this letter is being sent to others, please make a mention here.

Typist
Name of the typist and his initials at the bottom left of the letter.

Types of Government Letters
Broadly, government letters can be divided into two–
- Addressed to everyone
- Addressed to any specific department, institution or a person

Letters addressed to everyone may be about the following—
1. Notification
2. Oath
3. Declaration
4. Press Communiqué
5. Press Note
6. Ordinance
7. Correction & Corrigendum

8. Tender
9. Auction
10. Notice
11. Advertisement
12. General Government Letters
13. Semi-Government Letters
14. Circular
15. Memo/Official Memo
16. Office Order
17. Memorandum
18. Endorsement
19. Sanction Letter
20. Government Invitation Letters
21. Telegram

Notification

Notifications are very important form of communicatation of the government. The notifications are published in the Gazette. Notifications are also published in the newspapers for information to the general public. Upon publication, notifications acquire the legal status. These are written in the third person and don"t address any person as such. Name and designation of the person signing the notification is always mentioned.

Following are the different forms of notifications—

- ❏ Rules and regulations applicable for employees, ministries and departments are invariably published through notification.
- ❏ By notification, governments effect transfer of officers. Promotions, appointments and retirements are also published in the Gazette.
- ❏ Ministries notify their constitutional orders through notifications. Anonymous bodies and municipal corporations release a number of advertisements. Parliaments and State Assemblies make use of the notifications being communicated to the ordinary people.
- ❏ The Supreme Court, the High Courts, Railways, Banks, Law, Finance, Education departments or ministries can issue notifications.

In fact, notifications are a kind of order that is used to impart into operation by becoming various laws, rules and regulations.

(Sample-1)
Government of India
Ministry of Education

Sr. No…..   Notification   Date………

It is a form of information to the teaching community that teachers would be promoted only upon the submission of proofs of their Ph-D degree.

Designated certificate must be submitted to the authorised person in the department, failing which the appointment would become void.

Signature
Deputy Secretary

(Sample-2)
Government of India
Ministry of Finance, New Delhi

Sr. No…..   Notification   Date………

All pensioners are eligible to receive the enhanced Dearness Allowance of 6% like the regular employees. The pensioners are entitled to get the increased Dearness Allowance as applicable to regular employees.

Signature
Deputy Secretary

(Sample-3)
State Bank of India
New Delhi

Sr. No…..   Notification   Date………

On the direction of the Reserve Bank of India, all associate banks of the State Bank of India have been merged into the State Bank on India with effect from April 1, 2010. Controlling authorities of all associate banks are requested to complete the merger formalities by March 31, 2010.

Signature
Chief Manager

(Sample-4)
Government of India
Ministry of External Offices, New Delhi

Sr. No…..   Notification   Date………

As per the decision of the Government of India with effect from January 1, 20XX, all those who have acquired citizenship of the US and the UK, are eligible for dual citizenship provided they make an application in this regard. Last date for application is January 1, 20XX.

Applications will not be entertained thereafter.

Signature
Secretary
Ministry of External Office

(Sample-5)
Reserve Bank of India
New Delhi

Sr. No…..   Notification   Date………

It is for information that the Indian students pursuing studies abroad, whose parental income is below ₹ 20,000/- per month will not have to pay interest on education loan during the period of study. This will be borne by the government. The notification comes into force with immediate effect.

Governor
Reserve Bank of India

(Sample-6)
Government of India
Ministry of Agriculture

Sr. No…..   Notification   Date………

Vide reference no B-4/325/5, Deputy Secretary, Ministry of Agriculture Sri. Arun Bagle has been appointed as Director, in the Directors of Agriculture Marketing with effect from today.

Signature
Omkarnath Mishra
Government of India

Oath

An oath is resorted to whenever the government desires to consider any decision or controversial subject by any committee. It is also made use of in the case of appointing a commission or when the government desires to circulate the report of such a committee or commission for further consideration. An oath is always written in the third person and it doesn"t address anybody in particular.

A few samples are given ahead :

(Sample-1)

Ministry of Self-Employment
Government of Madhya Pradesh

Sr. No…..   Bhopal, Date………

The government has decided to appoint a committee to encourage the youth towards self-employment. There would be 3 nominees from the government and 5 from the non-government sectors.

Sri Shyamlal, MLA would head the committee. Following are the non-governmental members and their addresses :

    1………………
    2………………
    3………………
    4……………..

Names of the governmental nominees :

    1………………
    2………………
    3………………

A copy of the date be sent to each member of the committee, and published in the newspaper for due publicity.

The committee will submit its report within six months.

Secretary
Ministry of Self-Employment
Madhya Pradesh
Administration

(Sample-2)
Government of Madhya Pradesh
Ministry of Public Administration

Oath

(To be published in the official Gazette – part-II)

Date.......

The Madhya Pradesh administration is considering a proposal to merge a part of the Dearness Allowance being given to employees to the basic pay. A committee is being constituted composing of the following five members :

President of the committee...............

Members

1.....................
2.....................
3.....................
4.....................
5.....................

The committee will submit its report within four months.

Orders :

A copy of this oath is to be sent to each of the members of the committee, and should be published in the Gazette.

Signature
Deputy Secretary
Madhya Pradesh
Administration

Declaration

The government makes an announcement regarding the declaration whenever the President or the Governor has to address the nation on some important issue. The declaration is made only when the President or the Governor has appended his/her signature. Declaration of emergency, national mourning or creation of a new state are some of the examples that fall under this category. Declarations are published in the Gazette Extraordinary.

(Sample-1)
Declaration

There will be a state mourning for seven days following the death of…………..
minister, Sri…………of the ……………….state.

Governor
Madhya Pradesh

Date……..

(Sample-2)
Declaration

On account of the increasing terrorist activities, the citizens of India are suggested to remain vigilant and exercise caution while venturing out to public places. Should they discover anything suspicious, they must report to the police. Do not trust any stranger blindly and stay cautious during train/bus journey. This declaration is being published in all leading newspapers as well as our electronic media.

By order of the President
Signature
Under Secretary
Ministry of Home

Date………

Press Communiqué

A press communiqué is released in the interest of the general public. The press releases are generally published in the newspapers. Every government department has a public relations department. Public relations release news obtained from different departments of the ministry to newspapers for publication.

Press communiqué carries important happenings regarding steps taken to improve the lives of people, developmental activities, foreign collaboration, announcements by the Prime Minster, Chief Ministers and other important dignitaries. These are made available to the newspapers for due publicity.

A Press communiqué is prepared very cautiously since it reflects the government policies.

First of all, instructions are passed for publication on newspapers and the date on which this communiqué is to be published. Dates can"t be changed by the publishing newspaper. The communiqué carries the title of the text, releasing ministry or department, name, place and date, etc.

Name of the signatory and designation is also mentioned.

The releasing departments orders the public relations department to release the communiqué to the newspapers.

(Sample-1)
Press Communiqué
Office of the Executive Engineer
Electricity Department (West Zone, Indore)

The general public is informed that on account of maintenance work, electric supply to the west zone on January 5, 20XX between 12 noon to 4 pm. will be shut down. We regret the inconvenience caused.

Signature
Electrical Officer

Date.........

(Sample-2)
Office of the Commissioners
Municipal Corporation, Bhopal

The general public is hereby informed that water supply will remain shut for the whole of June 2, 20XX in the entire township. We regret the inconvenience being caused to the people during this period in the area.

Signature
Secretary
Municipal Corporation, Bhopal

Date.........

(Sample-3)
Madhya Pradesh Administration
Ministry of Transport, Bhopal

Through this press communiqué, we feel pleased to inform the citizens that in view of enormous difficulties being faced by them, while commuting, it has been decided to reintroduce plying of the State Road Transport buses. All arrangements have been made with effect from April 1, 20XX, for the buses to start plying as before.

Signature
Secretary
Transport Department

Date......

(Sample-4)
Commissioner
Delhi Development Authority, New Delhi

Vide letter No. 111, the general public is hereby informed that registration of plots will begin at 12 noon from February 2, 20XX in the office of the Delhi Development Authority and will continue to fill the allotment of plots. Interested persons may register their names by paying the requisite fees till January 28, 20XX. Only registered letters will be accepted.

Signature
Secretary, Delhi Development Authority

Date.......

(Sample-5)
Government of India
Ministry of Home Affairs

It is duly informed to the citizens of the State of Jammu & Kashmir that with a view to encourage people-to-people contact between the various nationals of India and Pakistan, visa requirements is being dispensed with. However a permit would, nevertheless be required to keep a tab on terrorist activities. This comes into effect from March 1, 20XX.

Under Secretary
Ministry of Home Affairs

Date.........

Press Note

The government makes use of a press note to inform the citizens of any important matter, news, happening, such as the impending impact of a visiting dignitary or to clarify any lingering doubt or confusion. Press notes are quite informal in comparison to press communiqué. If necessary, newspapers may edit them in accordance with the space available.

(Sample-1)

Press Note
Government of Uttar Pradesh
Ministry of Sports and Youth Affairs, Lucknow

Sr. No..........   Date.......

The Yuwa Mahotsava-12 is being organised in each district of the State from the 10th of August to the 20th August, 20XX. Students studying in any college situated within the state are eligible to take part. Programme details have been sent to all the colleges. If any college has not received the same, the programme schedule can be collected from the office of the district magistrate.

Public Relations Officer
Ministry of Sports & Youth Affairs
Secretary, Lucknow

(Sample-2)

Press Note
Government of Tamil Nadu
Department of Home Affairs, Chennai

The government of Tamil Nadu had eliminated the forces spread between the states of Tamil Nadu and Karnataka from the scourge of scandalous smugglers. Additional police forces have been deputed to guard the area. People can now live there freely and there is no need for them to abandon the area.

To be published in all the newspapers mentioned below.

Signature
Secretary, Home Affairs

(Sample-3)
Education Loan

The Ministry of Education, Government of Karnataka has sanctioned a scholarship of ₹ 1000/- per month to each research scholar engaged in science subjects besides earmarking a special educational loan to fulfil their needs. This educational loan would be disbursed by the banks in Karnataka on behalf of the government. For a study once in abroad for two years, a sum of ₹ 2 lakhs can be availed as loan. Those interested may apply to any scheduled bank, and for availing scholarship, please write to the Deputy Secretary (Education), Government of Karnataka, Bengaluru.

This facility is open to all those who are living in the State of Karnataka for the last five years. Please attach a documentary proof to this effect duly certified by the Collector of the district of residence. Applications will not be entertained in its absence.

Secretary
Education Department

Date…..

Ordinance

The power to (promulgate) ordinance lies with the President of India or the Governor of a State. Ordinance is normally promulgated on a subject of extreme importance and only at a time when the legislature is not in session. The Ordinance issued either by the President or the Governor expires automatically if not passed within a period of six weeks by Parliament or State Assembly respectively from the date of promulgation of the ordinance. The President or the Governor may resend the ordinance promulgated, if desired. The ordinance is published in the Gazette Extraordinary.

(Sample-4)
Ordinance
Government of India
Ministry of Law, New Delhi

Dated……..

Revocation of the Nationalisation of the General Insurance Ordinance takes place while the Parliament is not in session, and if the President is of the opinion that a situation of extreme importance has arisen to promulgate an Ordinance.

Under the powers granted under the section……. of the Constitution, the President has promulgated an Ordinance to take into effect immediately. The President is of the opinion that a situation of great importance has arisen, that necessitates promulgation of this Ordinance. Further, the parliament is in recess.

1. Name of the Ordinance
2. Area of Operation
3. Objective
4. Conditions

Correction and Corrigendum

Sometimes an error or two is deleted in the published Gazette. If it is deleted before being circulated, then a corrigendum is published in the same Gazette.

If the error is deleted after publication or when any modification becomes necessary, then a new Gazette is published showing the changes/corrections/modifications effected.

Corrections or modifications, as the case may be, are also published in the newspapers.

(Sample-1)
Government of Madhya Pradesh
Department Corrigendum Education

Sr. No……….   Bhopal, Dated……….

In the notification issued by the Ministry of Education vide serial no………… dated……………..which was published in the Gazette on………….., the name of the coordinator may be read as Sri Mohan Kumar Sharma instead of Sri Mohan Singh Sharma.

Under Secretary
Ministry of Education
Governor of Madhya Pradesh

Tender

Tenders are important documents. The governments limit commercial organisations or contractors for the submission of tenders. Following a set criteria, tenders are accepted for the purchase or execution of works. Tenders are very essential in the absence of which economic purchases can not be made. If the tendering process is not undertaken, allegations of favouratism or nepotism surface and may end in court cases. Following are the examples of tenders :

(Sample-1)

Telephone Nigam Limited, New Delhi

The process of laying underground wiring for telephone is going on since last year. Now they have planned to operate it automatically. Technical bids are being invited for execution of this work. Bids would be accepted on official forms only, which can be from this office.

Forms will not be available after the last date mentioned herein. Forms completed in all respects are to be submitted by the 25th January, 20XX to the designated authority either in person or by registered post. Only those can apply who have an experience of executing government projects for five years or more.

Tenderers have to submit proofs that their income tax returns are up-to-date.

The value of the tender is around ₹ 5 crores. The work has to be completed within three months from the date of winning the tender. An amount of ₹ 1 lakh need to be deposited as a form of security at the time of submission of the tender forms. Those whose tenders are rejected will have their security deposit refunded.

The tenders will be opened on February 1, 20XX at 2 pm by a committee consisting of three engineers of the telephone department. Kindly deposit the security money through a D/D of the State Bank of India to the Chief Engineer, Telephones, New Delhi.

Tenders may be rejected without assigning any reason.

Engineer-in-charge
Telephones, New Delhi

Date………..

(Sample-2)

Sometimes tenders are invited for a number of items within the same bid document. Date and time of the submission is indicated therein. Descriptions regarding the evaluation process is also mentioned.

Superintendent, Police

Lucknow, Uttar Pradesh

All police stations in Uttar Pradesh are being modernised. Police inspectors in every police station are being provided with a laptop. Tenders are invited from interested parties, particulary from the computer firms. Prices of the following items have to be mentioned by the tenders :

1. Laptop
2. Printer
3. Scanner

About 300 police stations are to be provided with these. The infrastructure for the creation of a working place is also to be created by the tenderers.

Date................   Signature
                                                                        Superintendent, Police

Important Points

1. Submit your bid on official tender form within seven days of the date of publication of the tender.
2. Quota for setting up infrastructure and equipments separately.
3. Earnest money of ₹ 50,000/- is to be deposited by way of security.
4. In case, the bid is rejected, the amount would be refunded by deducting ₹ 5000/-
5. In case of disputes, a court in Lucknow will have the final jurisdiction.

Date...   Superintendent, Police
                                                                                Lucknow

Auction

An auction is the process by which government departments dispose of items or products that they can"t make use of effectively and usefully. Such information is published in the newspapers. Auction information is released in two forms with full information given out in the newspapers. In the next, brief information about the items being put up for auction is published in the newspapers along with the name and address of the department concerned.

(Sample-1)

Auction Notice

The general public is hereby informed that the process of auctioning forest produce of the district of Indore will take place on………at…………..at the Forest Conservation Office, Indore.

Detailed information about the auction may be had from the office of the Forest Conservation, Indore during the working hours.

Forest Conservation
Indore

Notice

Accurate information is of vital importance while writing, both in the governmental and non-governmental correspondence. The government makes public, the required information through the press. If necessary, posters and banners are also pasted at high visibility points. Notices are of various kinds.

A few samples are:

(Sample-1)

Awards for Information Regarding Prisoners Escaped from Jail

The Ministry of Home Affairs, Government of Kerala, Thiruvananthapuram has announced a reward of ₹ 2 lakh for the information regarding three prisoners who escaped from the jail last week. Their sketches have been circulated over the local TV channels. Information regarding them may be passed on to the nearest police station.

An award each of ₹ 2 lakhs will be given to the person for helping the police arrest the prisoners.

Date……   Published by the Government of Kerala

(Sample-2)
No Action against Striking Employees

The government of Rajasthan has announced that those staff of the Sales Tax Department who went on strike last week, will not have their salaries deducted or sacked from service, if they rejoin their duties within three days and enter into discussion to solve the problem at hand. Those who don"t do will be suspended and stringent action taken against them.

Date..........   Secretary
                                                                                         Department of Sales Tax

---

(Sample-3)
Education Department, Indore

The Navin College, Indore has been allotted around 5 acres of land near Khajrana for the construction of its campus. This land belongs to the government but, many individuals have put forward their claims on it. Such individuals are requested to submit their claims along with proofs of ownership, failing which their claims will be considered null and void.

The government has filed a case in the court. In case, no objection is received, construction of the college campus will commence.

Date............   Additional Controller
                                                                                   Education Department, Indore

---

(Sample-4)
Government of India
Department of Administrative Affairs

The government of India has appointed the 6th Pay Commission, which is likely to submit its report by March 2009.

The government has decided to raise the retirement age of the government staff from 62 to 65 for the staff of the Education Department. This will offer employment to the youth and at the same time allow for experienced hands to contribute their valuable knowledge and expertise.

The government has set up a fund for the transfer of eligible amount into the pension portfolio. It will begin from the day of joining service and deposited into the personal account of each employee.

This is being circulated through the newspapers for due publicity.

Dated............   Secretary

(Sample-5)
**Controller of Information and Statistical Division,
Government of Madhya Pradesh, Bhopal
Change of Address**

The general public is hereby informed that the office of information and Statistical Division has shifted from the erstwhile office at Sadar Manzil, Bhopal to Paryavaran Bhawan, 1st Floor, B-Sector, Jail Road with effect from January 1, 20XX.

Controller
Information & Statistical Division
Government of Madhya Pradesh, Bhopal

Advertisement

The government releases advertisement :
1. When vacancies are to be filled with suitable candidates
2. To publicise any of its activities
3. Calling for applications for scholarships
4. To publicise about government publications

The same advertising process in applied whenever any autonomous body calls to fill vacancies on behalf of the government or any to its department.

Examples are given below:

**(Sample-1)
Kendriya Shiksha Board
Ramkrishnapuram, New Delhi**

Applications are invited for the following posts lying vacant in the Kendriya Shiksha Board.

Post	Salary	No. of Vacancies	Reservations
Asst. Director	5000-200-1500	10	2
Translator	4000-150-10000	20	5

Dearness Allowance, as applicable is also payable. Age and educational qualification are as under:
1. Age should be between 22 to 35 at the time of making applications.
2. For Assistant Director, a minimum of MA and for the translator at least a Graduate with Hindi and English as subjects.

Notification

3. Experience – For Assistant Director – 1 year and for Translator – 2 years

Please submit the application in the format given below and sent it to the Officer Administration, Kendriya Shiksha Board, Ramkrishnapuram, New Delhi within 10 days. Applications received after this date will not be entertained.

Format :
1. Name of the Post
2. Name and Address
3. Date of Birth
4. Nationality
5. Marital Status
6. Educational Qualifications
7. Do you belong to the reserved category?

Passport Size Photo

Examination	Board/University	Year of Passing	Division	Subjects
1	2	3	4	5
(1)				
(2)				
(3)				

8. Experience

Company Name	Post & Scale	From to	Nature of Work Reason for Leaving
1	2	3	4

9. Interests
10. Are you prepared to serve anywhere in India?
11. Any other relevant information
12. A certificate that all the information given above are true to the best of my knowledge and belief.

Date.......
Place.......   Signature

Applications are sent in the format prescribed. There is no need to send another application. There days a CV is sent to the concerned department calling for applications for specific posts. Online applications are also invited by many organisations.

Applications in specific formats make it easy to short-list applications of eligible candidates.

(Sample-2)

Following is the prescribed format in which applications are to be sent.

Last date for the applications to reach office – 2/3/20XX

Punjab National Bank, Amritsar

Advertisement No................ Date.........

(1) Officer – 1. Grade A
             2. Officer – Grade B

(2) Examination Centre
     Serial Number

(3) Details of D/D or Postal Order

Name of the Bank   D/D No   Amount

(4) Name

(5) Date of Birth

(6) Address

(7) Category to which one belongs (Tick one)

General   Scheduled Caste   Scheduled Tribe   Other Backward Classes

Ex-Serviceman – Yes/No

Employee in this organisation – Yes/No

(8) Permanent Address

(9) Educational Qualifications

S. No.	Examinations Passed	Board/University & Year of Passing	Subjects and Percentage
(1)			
(2)			
(3)			

(10) Experience if any

(11) Did you apply for pre-selection training – Yes/No

(12) I certify that all the information given above are in line to the best of my knowledge and belief. If any information is found to be wrong, my appointment may be terminated at any time. I have read and understood the terms and conditions of the examination.

Place........... Signature
Date........... Name

Correspondence of the Ordinary Government

Ordinary or general governmental correspondence relate to those letters that is written by the government of India to the state government and vice versa or among the state governments or any department, autonomous bodies or individuals. These letters are very formal. The language used is simple and polite.

Different ministries of a government instead of writing an official letter, make use of a note. The common format of the governmental correspondence is given below:

(Sample-1)

The Government of India
Ministry of Human Resources
Letter No..............
Sender
Deputy Secretary
Government of India, New Delhi

Sir,

It has been decided that the educational policy should be uniform in all the schools throughout the country. As a matter of fact, school curriculum should have been made uniform much earlier. It has been decided that all the schools will use the mother tongue of the state for teaching in the schools.

If you could legislate in your State Assembly and send it within three months, the parliament would be able to pass a bill making the school curriculum uniform throughout the country.

Soliciting your cooperation in this matter,

Yours faithfully,
Deputy Secretary
Ministry of Human Resources, New Delhi

Encl: Copy to all the state governments

(Sample-2)

The Government of Uttar Pradesh
Ministry of Home Affairs, Lucknow
Sr. No……..   Date……..

Sender	Copy
Chief Secretary (Home)	Chief Secretary (Home
Government of India, New Delhi	The Government of Uttar Pradesh, Lucknow

Subject: Challenge of Terrorism

Sir,

    It has come to the notice of the Intelligence Bureau that a number of terrorist organisations are active in the state of Uttar Pradesh and have plans to make use of explosions to disturb the peace and harmony among various communities. Further they might carry out their nefarious designs on important ministers. Please remain vigilant and extend your cooperation to the Central Bureau of Investigation (CBI).

Yours faithfully
Chief Secretary (Home)
New Delhi

(Sample-3)

Department of General Administration
Government of Madhya Pradesh, Bhopal

Sender	Copy
Under Secretary	All District Magistrates
General Administration, Bhopal	Madhya Pradesh

Sir,

    It is brought to your notice that instructions and suggestions of the general administration department is being overlooked and works are not executed the way they should have. You are directed to ensure compliance that every staff reports to the office in time, otherwise the onus will be on district magistrates.

    If necessary, resort to surprise checks.

Yours faithfully,
Signature

Notification

Besides general administration letters, sometimes letters are exchanged between two departments. There letters are written in the manner of general correspondence but are limited to just one specific case.

A few examples are given below:

(Sample-4)
Government of Gujarat
Gandhi Nagar

Sir,

The grant sanctioned to our cooperative unit this year is much less then that of previous years. As such, we are not able to meet the required expenditure. Most works will remain held up until additional funding is made available. Hence additional grants may be sanctioned as that of the previous years.

Yours faithfully
Pankaj Patel
Rajya Sahkari Sanstha
Ahmedabad

(Sample-5)
Government of Bihar, Patna

Copy
Sri Prakash Mishra
Deputy Secretary, Railway Board
New Delhi
Sr. No.   Date:............

Subject : Broad Guage Lines Allottment of Funds

Sir,

The Ministry of Railways has informed us that the decision regarding conversion of the metre guage lines into broad guage (passing through Bihar) has been taken. We have not received its copy so far. Kindly expedite the process so that the lines are uniformly converted into broad guage at the earliest.

Yours sincerely,
Ram Singh, Secretary
Bihar Railway Board, Patna

(Sample-6)
Government of India
Ministry of External Affairs

Ministry of Foreign Affairs
New Delhi

Copy
High Commissions
India High Commission
Great Britain

Subject : Visa Regulations

Sir,

Please take up the issue with the U.K. government that the planned modification in the visa roles don"t adversely affect the indians visiting U.K. The India government is prepared to issue a certificate to the Non-resident Indians so as to prevent the illegal migrants from entering U.K. The move, has been planned to be brought into effect by the U.K. government, could imperil the prospects of genuine Indians.

Keep us informed of new developments.

Thanking you,

Sr. No :..........
Date :............

Yours faithfully,
Secretary

(Sample-7)
Government of NCT of Delhi

The Secretary
Ministry of Home Affairs, Government of India
New Delhi

Sr :..........
Date :.......

Subject : Additional Police Force

Sir,

Incidence of crime continues to rise its ugly head in the Capital. The Delhi government doesn"t have adequate police force at its command. You are requested to earmark two battalions of police force on an urgent basis.

Yours faithfully,
Secretary Home
Government of NCT of Delhi

(Sample-8)
Government of India
Department of Languages, New Delhi

Date:.........

Sri Azad Singh
Director, Languages Deptartment, New Delhi

Subject : Promotion of National Languages

Sir,
It had been found that proper translation of important documents is not been rendered by the Hindi Officers. Officers of concerned departments have expressed dissatisfaction on this matter. You are requested to take immediate action to improve the translations.

Yours faithfully,
Pronoy Ray
Deputy Secretary
Languages, New Delhi

Demi-official Letter

Demi-official letters also from part of official correspondence. Only difference being that such letters are less formal and reflect a personal equation between the sender and the receiver.

Demi-official letters are written when an official wants to draw the attention of the recipient to an important issue or to any long pending matter. These letters often elicit immediate response. Such letters begin with some respectable salutation.

(Sample-1)
Demi-official Letter Serial No.

Date:........

Principal,
Government Postgraduate College
Bhopal (M.P.)

Dear Dr. Advani,
I had sent you a letter dated....... inviting you to participate during the inaugural function of the commerce council of the college. I hope you must be in receipt of the letter.
Kindly oblige me by confirming your participation.
Regards,

Yours sincerely,
Ratan Sharma

(Sample-2)
Government of Uttar Pradesh
Ministry of Home Affairs

Sr. No.   Date:........

Subject : Need for Strong Effective Laws against Terrorism

Dear Sir,

I hope you are hale and hearty. I agree with your belief that terrorism is on the rise in India. Time has come when we need to take strong measures to improve the internal security matter than pandering to the vote bank politics. You have to pass strong legislative laws to counter the threat, just administrative actions will not be enough.

My contention is that the western concept of human rights doesn"t quite apply in this country. We are trying to check the evils of communalism. There exist a number of misconceptions within the communities. Now even the U.S. and Europe are suffering the wrath of terrorism and are bringing forward tough laws against them.

There is an urgent need to begin with to issue an ordinance to this effect, failing which new problems will keep cropping up. I regret, we are not able to protect the freedom of the media. This is sending wrong signals to the rest of the world.

We may belong to different political parties, but we all seek the welfare of the nation. The Prime Minister"s exhortation regarding stronger action against terrorism is commendable. I have requested the Home Ministers of other states to write to you on this important matter.

Regards,

Yours sincerely,
Home Minister
Uttar Pradesh

Copy:
Home Minister, Government of India, New Delhi

(Sample-3)
**Office of the District Magistrate
Gwalior**

Sr. No:.........
Dated:.........

Dear Sir,

    You are requested to kindly keep my transfer-on-hold for at least six months, as I have been able to control the anti-social elements after many efforts and now my attention is to check the menace of dacoity. If I am transferred, the initiative would be lost.

    I get the feeling that my transfer has been effected due to pressure from some higher authorities. Kindly look into the said order and try to get it rescinded.

Yours sincerely,
Rajpal Singh
District Magistrate, Gwalior

Copy:
Smt. Shalini Devi
Chief Secretary
Government of Madhya Pradesh, Bhopal

Circular

    Circulars are used as a medium to communicate any information, news, order or other important matters to a number of individuals or departments. The sender and the subject matter remain the same but the recipients are different.

    Some examples of circulars are given below :

(Sample-1)
Government of Madhya Pradesh
Ministry of Social Welfare
Ballabh Bhawan, Bhopal, M.P.

Sr. No:………..   dated:…………

The Honourable Governor of Madhya Pradesh works to know the number of Scheduled Tribe members, who are are posted as Gazetted officers in all the districts of Madhya Pradesh.

Kindly furnish the required information at the earliest.

Surendra Singh
Deputy Secretary
Ministry of Social Welfare
Bhopal, M.P.

Copy :
All District Magistrates
Madhya Pradesh

Memo/Official Memo

Most popular form of communication among government, non-government and other administrative departments is through memo. These are free from most official formalities, such as names of the sender and receiver or salutation.

Memos are mostly used on the following occasions:
- Acknowledgement of receipt of a letter
- Replies to request letters
- Communications necessary to give the appropriate directions to the subordinate staff.

(Sample-1)
Office of the Principal
S.V. Polytechnic, Bhopal

Sr. No:............   Date

Sri Suresh Narayan, Grade-III, Mechanical Engineering Department has been granted leave of 15 days as desired by him with effect from............out of his earned leave account.

Signature
Principal
S.V. Polytechnic, Bhopal

Copy:
1. Head of Mechanical Engineering
2. Accounts Officer
3. Establishment Section
4. Sri Suresh Narayan, Assistant Grade-III
   For information and necessary action

(Sample-2)
Government of Dayanand Saraswati College
Ujjain (M.P.)

Sr. No:............   Date:.........

With reference to his letter dated........., Sri Anil Sharma is directed to report to the undersigned on............at 11.00 in the morning.

Principal
Government Dayanand Saraswati College
Ujjain

(Sample-3)
Government of Madhya Pradesh
Ministry of Finance

Sr. No:............... Bhopal, Date...........
All Heads of the Departments &
All District Magistrates
Madhya Pradesh

Subject : Regarding Allowances Payable on Transfer

Accountant General, Madhya Pradesh has drawn the attention of this department towards the unauthorised claims of certain government employees while being transferred from one place to another. Kindly ensure that there are no unauthorised claims which have been made before countersigning the form/5.

Deputy Secretary
Ministry of Finance
Government of Madhya Pradesh

Copy :
Secretary, Revenue Board
Secretary, Madhya Pradesh Public Service Commission
Secretary, Madhya Pradesh Vidhan Sabha
All Finance & Accounts Officers, Madhya Pradesh for information and necessary action.

Office Order

Any order issued with regard to any work related to office, such as ads, appointments, transfers, confirmations in the jobs, etc are known as office orders. A copy of this order is sent to the concerned department. Following are some of the samples of office orders :

(Sample-1)
Office Order
Office of the Madhya Pradesh Public Service, Madhya Pradesh

Sr. No:………..
Date:…………..

It has been decided that any candidate, who upon selection, joins his/her duty to the designated post, will be entitled to oppear for the examinations conducted by the Madhya Pradesh Public Service Commission upto a maximum of three times. This order comes into effect from the 1st of September, 20XX.

Signature
Secretary
M.P. Public Service Commission
Madhya Pradesh

Copy :
1. All Ministries of the M.P. Government
2. Publicity offer, Public Service Commission for Information and for Publicity in all leading Newspapers.

(Sample-1)
Memorandum
Office of District Education Officer, Jaipur

Sr. No:..............   Jaipur
From   Date:.
Sri Avanindra Jajoo, M.Com, Ph-D.
District Education Office
Jaipur

Divisional Education Officer
Jaipur Division
Jaipur

Subject : Secondary Examination

Ref: This Office Letter No………………..   dated…………..

Sir,

   Your kind attention is drawn to the fact that the secondary examinations are commencing soon, but the question papers have not arrived so far.

   Kindly ensure that the question papers are dispatched at the earliest.

Yours faithfully,
Avanindra Jajoo
District Education Officer
Jaipur

(Sample-2)
Memo, Government of Madhya Pradesh
Ministry of Home Affairs

Sr. No................   Bhopal, Date:...........

The undersigned is directed to ascertain the date by which reply to this office memo no. ....dt...............would by received in this office.

Dinesh Kumar
Dy. Secretary
Ministry of Home Affairs
Government of Madhya Pradesh

Superintendent of Police
District–Indore

Endorsement

Endorsement is a kind of memo. When an endorsement letter is received in an office then by the way of acknowledgement to the sender or to circulate among the office staff, the method of endorsement is used. A copy of the original letter is used for circulation.

It can be done in two ways—endorsement with comments/remarks or without. When endorsement is made with comments, the comments should be brief.

Endorsement is used for the following:
1. For initiating necessary action
2. For forwarding views and comments
3. For replying to the sender
4. For information

Normally, the endorsement exhibits the following. On the top is mentioned the serial number, the name of the office endorsing the letter. This is followed by the date of endorsement and to whom it is being sent. Name and dispensation of the person endorsing the letter.

The following note is written while endorsing a letter.

Original/Copy of letter No.................sent for information/necessary action.

Sample of Endorsement:

Endorsement
Government of Uttar Pradesh
Ministry of Education

Endorsement No:..................   Lucknow, Date:........

The copy of Ministry of Human Resources, Government of India, New Delhi letter No……………..is sent to the following for information and necessary action—
1. All District Magistrates in Uttar Pradesh
2. All Government Colleges in Uttar Pradesh
3. All Non-government Colleges in Uttar Pradesh

Encl: As above

Signature
Dy. Secretary
Ministry of Education, Uttar Pradesh

Sanction Letter

As per the Constitution of India, the President is the head of the Executive. The position of the Governor in a state corresponds to the one enjoyed by the President of the Union. No order within a State takes effect without the signature of the Governor. It is not always possible to obtain the signature of the Governor. The statute has granted subjects on which the signature of the President/Governor, as the case may be, is necessary. Such letters are called Sanction Letters.

Following are some of the samples of sanction letters:

(Sample-1)
Government of Madhya Pradesh
Department of Higher Education

Sr. No:……………   Bhopal, Date:………..

Registrar
Department of Higher Education
Madhya Pradesh

**Subject : Opening of a New College in Village Kala Peepal,
District Shajapur**

Sir,

    The undersigned is directed to convey that the Governor has sanctioned opening of a new college in village Kala Peepal in Shajapur district.

    The expenses on this account may be reflected in the Account No. 40

By order of the Governor of Madhya Pradesh
Deputy Secretary
Department of Higher Education, Madhya Pradesh

Sr. No:………   Bhopal, Date:………..

    A copy of the order (together with four extra copies) sent to the Finance Department and Accountant General, Gwalior for information and necessary action.

(Sample-2)
Government of Madhya Pradesh
Department Linguistics

Sr. No:…………..   Bhopal, Date:………..

Registrar
Department of Linguistics, Madhya Pradesh
Bhopal

Subject : Sri Azad Reddy, Hindi Officer, Dept. of Linguistics, Madhya Pradesh, Bhopal
For grant of Special Allowance

In exercise of powers granted under the Madhya Pradesh Special Rules Section………Sub-Section……….., Sri Azad Reddy, Hindi Officer, Dept. of Linguistics, Bhopal is sanctioned a special allowance of 10% over and above his pay and allowances.

By order of the Governor of Madhya Pradesh
Secretary
Dept. of Linguistics
Governor of Madhya Pradesh

Copy :
1. Finance Department, Madhya Pradesh
2. Accountant General, Madhya Pradesh, Gwalior
3. Sri Azad Reddy, Hindi Office, Department of Linguistics for information & necessary action.

Dy. Secretary
Department of Linguistics
Government of Madhya Pradesh

Official Invitation Letter

Invitation letters are issued by Government Departments, Governors, Chief Ministers, other Ministers or other Government Officers on the occasion of significance or during important functions.

Sample of Official Invitation Letters
Official Invitation Letter

Sri (Name of Governor), The Governor of Madhya Pradesh and
Smt. ……………..(wife of Governor) invite
Name and address of the invitee
On the occasion of……………………
at place & address …………………………on weekday, (the date and time)
……………………………………………………
……………………………………………………..
……………………………………………………..

(Sample-3)

Government of Maharashtra
Minister of (Name of the Department)

Pleased to invite
Name and address of the invitee
On the occasion of …………………..
at (Address + Place) on ……………. weekday, the …………..date……..
at time…………………

Telegram

When a message is to be delivered cogently, a telegram is sent. Use of telegram shows the important and cogency of communication. Since sending a telegram is expensive where each word used is to be paid, brevity becomes very important. Grammatical rules are done away with.

Telegrams are of two kinds
1. Plain Telegram
2. Diplomatic Telegram

Plain Telegram

Telegrams that use plain and simple words are known as plain telegrams. Anyone receiving this can understand its contents.

Diplomatic Telegram

These are of two kinds :

1. Ordinary Telegram
2. Express Telegram

Governments classify telegrams according to the significance and cogency of the communication.

Classification:

1. SOS (Save Our Soul) Life-Saving
2. Lightening
3. Military Lightning
4. Urgent (Express)
5. Ordinary

Except for the diplomatic telegrams, copies of all other telegrams are confirmed by ordinary mails by the sender. There are no signatures of the senders on telegrams. Confirmatory copies bear the senders" signatures.

Forms of Telegrams

1. The wire, Telegram is placed on the top priority.
2. In the next line of classification of telegrams is written as ordinary, express, urgent and lightning.
3. Name and address of the receiver.
4. Contents of the telegram. It is written between two lines.
5. Name and designation of the sender.
6. For information of telegraph office — After the name of the sender is written, a long horizontal line is drawn below in which the words, 'Not to be telegraphed" is written. Below this the name, designations signatures, office address, etc. are written (For record purposes only).

Following are some of the samples of telegrams :

(Sample-1)

Telegram　　　　　　　　Government　　　　　　　　Urgent

Chief Secretary
Ministry of Education
Bhopal (M.P.)
Reply urgently to this office letter No...................dt.........................

Deputy Secretary
Ministry of Human Resources
New Delhi

(Sample-2)

Government Telegram

All departments are informed that the chief minister"s visit is cancelled.

Copy to :	Secretary
Confirmatory copy to	Governor of Rajasthan
all concerned Departments	Jaipur
Date:..........	

Section – 8
Receipt and Dispatch of Letters

Receipt & Dispatch Department and its Importance

Every government department has a department which receives and dispatches letters. This department keeps record of all letters that arrive or are sent out.

The section that records the incoming mail is known as the *receipt section* and the section dispatching mails is known as the *dispatch section*.

Importance

The Receipt and Dispatch sections are a vital component of any office. Their main function is delivering letters, received from outside, to the concerned authorities in a timely manner. If not distributed in time, many impinge on the reputation of the office. Same goes for the dispatch section also.

Working of the receipt and the dispatch section.

These are divided into two sections :

1. Incoming mails
2. Outgoing mails

Process followed for incoming mails

These letters are the ones that have been received from outside.

1. Receipt of letters
2. Opening of letters
3. Making entry into the receipt register with docket number for identification
4. Separating into different departments
5. Sending letters to concerned departments

Recurring Letters

An employee is allotted a table and space where mails from outside are received. This person receives mails and acknowledges them.

Quite often, large departments even send their concerned employee to the post office to collect letters on their behalf. Some offices maintain a box number with a post office. Letters are dropped into the post box by the postal staff. Such letters, instead of full address of the office only have the post box and name of the city/town written on the letter.

Opening of Letters

There are two kinds of letters. One – personal letters of employees and the other, official. Envelopes containing personal letters are delivered to the concerned person, unopened, whereas the official ones are opened, duly locked into the incoming receipt register and forwarded to the concerned official.

Making Entry of the Incoming Mails into the Register and Docketing

After opening mails, their entry is made into a register. This register has the following columns.

1. Serial number
2. Date of receipt of the letter
3. Sender"s reference no. and date
4. Address of the sender
5. Subject
6. Any special information, remarks

Sr. No.	Date of receipt	Sender"s Reference No. and Date	Address of the Sender	Subject	Remarks
1	2	3	4	5	6

After making an entry in the register in the above manner, a seal is stamped on the front face of the received mail.

The seal indicates the following:

1. Name of the receiving office
2. Date of receipt
3. Receipt serial number
4. Time of receipt
5. To whom forwarded
6. Signature of the receiving staff

This process is called *docketing*.

Separating letters as per the Department

Once docketing has been done, letters are separated according to the department. Thereafter, these mails are entered into the internal Dak delivery diary. Internal dak delivery diary contains four columns. They are :

1. Serial number of the letter (mail)
2. Name of the official to whom the letter is being forwarded
3. Signature of the official to whom the letter has been forwarded
4. Remarks

After making entry into the internal dak delivery diary, the letter is forwarded to the concerned official and his signature obtained. Then the head of the office is informed to the official concerned and his signature is obtained. Afterwards, th head of the office is informed of the delivery status of the received mails.

Outgoing Letters

Every letter sent out reflects the personality of the office. Letters are expected to improve relations, business and productivity. Outgoing letters are of two kinds. One that represent replies to a previous received mail and another a fresh letter from a department to someone else. Following procedure is followed:

1. Receipt of mail from various departments into receipt and dispatch section.
2. Making entry of the outgoing mails into the dispatch register.
3. Putting into the envelope and writing of the addressee (Name and Address).
4. Pasting of postage stamp
5. Dispatch of letters

Following entries are made into the outgoing register:

Sr. No.	Date	Name & Address of the receiver	Subject	Enclo-sures	Method of Dispatch	Value of Postage Stamp	Remarks
1	2	3	4	5	6	7	8

Placing Letters inside the Envelopes

Reference numbers are marked on the letters and then entries in the outgoing register is made. Address of the receiver is written on the envelope before letters are put and issued. Name and address of the sending office is mentioned on the left bottom side of the envelope. If the addressee is not found, the envelope calls for it to be returned to the sending office. On top of the envelope, the reference number of the letter is indicated.

Affixing Postage Stamps on the Envelope

Postage stamps are pasted on the envelope according to the weight and method of dispatch –registered or ordinary. This is done by the post office through which letters are being sent. After affixing the postage stamp on the envelopes, the postal office, makes entries in the dak dispatch diary along with the value of postage under the following columns:

Date	Opening Balance	Amount of Postage used	Types of Letters	Name of the Addressee	Balance Amount Remaining
1	2	3	4	5	6

The dak dispatch diary gives details of the opening balance of the amount (of value of postage stamps) postage stamps issued that day, type and letters, address of the receiver and the balance standing in the name of the particular dispatching office.

Letters sent by Post Office or by Hand/Courier

Letters that are to be sent by the Post Office are dropped inside the post box. Letters to be sent by a persons/couriers are given to them after making due entries in to the diary. The courier delivers letters at the destination and hands back the acknowledgements obtained from the recipients to the sender.

Sr. No.	Date	Dispatch Ref No. & Date	Addressee	Name of the Courier	Signature of the Addressee	Remarks
1	2	3	4	5	6	7

The government makes use of the postal department besides courier to send letters and parcels. Postage don"t have to be affixed on packets sent by courier. Instead of a fixed sum is paid to them according to their tariff. These days extensive use of courier services are being made by commercial organisations to send their letters.

Office

Office-How They Work

Office is a place to get a job done in a planned way.

Every organisation, whether a school, college, collectorate or secretariat, financial organisation, commercial unit, factory or sales-point, needs an office to regulate its scheduled work.

Description of an Office

Indexing the various kinds of works an office has to perform is a difficult job because different institutions provide different kinds of solutions and therefore, their book keeping varies. However, there are basic infrastructure requirements, each office has to have:

1. Information gathering
2. Collection of information
3. Compilation of information for proper execution
4. Safety of information
5. Supply of information

Information Gathering

Gathering information about the organisation is an important function of that unit. There are basically two sources for gathering information – outside sources and internal sources. Sometimes, information is received orally. Other forms of gathering information are governmental and non-governmental letters, as also from commercial establishments, supplies and customer letters.

Compilation of Information/News

Information gathered from various sources is compiled and then segregated into different files as per the need. Attempts are made to gather information that are not forthcoming easily.

Analysis of Information

Information gathered is analysed so that decisions could be made on the basis of such findings. Based on the sales and purchase information, future purchasing policies could be made. On the basis of complaints received from the customers, servicing policies could be modified.

Security of Information

Information gathered and analysed are to be protected from leakage. This is an important duty of the organisation.

Exchange of Information

Exchanging information with various stakeholders is one of the pivotal functions of any office. The functions that an office has to perform are as under:

- Planning the work schedule of the office
- Management control
- Planning for optimal use
- Public relations
- Security of infrastructure
- Executing social responsibilities

Influence of Correspondence

Letters are an important contributory function of any organisation/office. Nearly 90% of the information that accumulates at an office is through the medium of letters or various modes of correspondence/communication. Different kinds of notices, circulars, orders, etc. are communicated through the means of letters. These days *e-mails* have come into being. It means *electronic mails*. A lot of salutary symbolisms are done away with in *e-mails*. In fact, writing letters is the fulcrum on which the balance of any office is hinged. Security of correspondence and maintaining a copy of every single mail are the essential duties of an office.

Section – 9
Bank and E-mail Letters

Bank-related Correspondence

Banks have a unique identity in the society. Every now and then, we have to correspond with them on a number of issues. We need to write to them when trying to open a new account with the bank, requisitioning a new cheque book, informing them of the loss of a cheque leaf or a book, enquiring about a locker, payment of utility bills, such as, telephone, electricity, closing an account or for transacting a large amount.

A few examples are given below:

Refusal by a Bank to Honour a Cheque
Punjab National Bank

23, Bhogal
New Delhi – 110014

Sri Hukam Singh
5, Bhogal
New Delhi – 110014

Dear Sir,

We would like to draw your kind attention to the cheque no. 456732 dated.... for ₹ 2000/- issued by Sri Kamal Diwan which you had deposited for crediting into your account.

We regret to inform you that the signature doesn"t match the record maintained by the bank; and therefore, it is being returned to you.

Yours faithfully,
Manmohan Singh
Manager

Encl: One cheque mentioned above

Stop Payment Instruction

Name and address of the sender
Dated:

The Manager
Oriental Bank of Commerce
Paschim Vihar, New Delhi – 110063

Sub: Request to Stop Payment

Dear Sir,

I had issued a cheque bearing number 797623 dated.... for ₹ 5,000/- in favour of Sri Manav Kulkarni.

Last night, I was telephonically informed about the loss of the said cheque.

You are requested not to honour the cheque.

Thanking you,

Yours faithfully,
Name and Address

Letter to a Party Complaining about Bouncing of its Cheque
Vijay Vastra Bhandar

Address
Dated:

Messrs. Nirmal Textiles
18, Nangloi, New Delhi

Dear Sir,

We regret to inform you that the cheque (cheque no: 372947) for ₹ 1,000/- you had issued in our favour has been returned to us by our banker, 'State Bank of India" citing the reason of 'for want of funds". The cheque in question is enclosed for your reference.

Kindly arrange to pay the above amount at the earliest.

Yours faithfully,
Pankaj Malhan
Manager

Encl: One cheque mentioned above

Letter to Issue a Passbook

Address of the sender
Dated:

The Manager
Canara Bank
Lakkad Bazaar, Ulhas Nagar

Sub: Request to Issue a Duplicate Passbook

Dear Sir,

I maintain one S/B A/C no- 38497648498875 with your bank. I have misplaced my original Passbook. In its absence, I am unable to know the transactions made; and the balance remaining in my account.

I request you to issue me a duplicate passbook.

Thanking you,

Yours faithfully,
Name

Request to Open a Bank Locker A/C

Address of the sender
Dated:

The Manager
Navjivan Bank
Shakti Nagar, Badlapur

Sub: Request to Open a Bank Locker A/C

Dear Sir,

For the last four years, I have been maintaining a Recurring Deposit A/C (R/D A/C No...). Now I am in an urgent need to open a Bank Locker A/C to keep my documents and other valuables safely and securely. I request you to enlighten me with the rules and regulations governing the bank locker.

Thanking you,

Yours faithfully,
Name

Letter by a Bank Demanding Regular Payment of Monthly Instalments against Loan Advanced
State Bank of India

20, Karol Bagh
New Delhi – 110005
Dated:

Sri Praveen Dixit
133 B, Patel Nagar
New Delhi – 110008

Sub: Regarding Timely and Regular Deposit of Monthly Instalments

Dear Sir,

This is to bring to your kind notice that a loan of ₹ 30,000/- was advanced by this branch to you for purchase of household furniture. By your letter dated…, you had assured us to repay the loan amount with interest thereon @ ₹ 1,000/- every month. Unfortunately, you have failed to do so.

We request you to arrange for the payment of monthly instalments in time, failing which action may be initiated against you.

Yours faithfully,
For State Bank of India
Manager

Application for Housing Loan

Address
Dated

The Manager
Syndicate Bank
Paharganj
New Delhi

Sub: Housing Loan Required

Dear Sir,

    I am working in the Navodaya Vidyalaya as Principal; and maintain a S/B A/C No….. with your bank. Please let me know the formalities and the terms and conditions towards obtaining a housing loan.

    Thanking you,

Yours faithfully,
Name

Closure of S/B A/C

Address
Dated

The Manager
Allahabad Bank

Shivaji Park, Mumbai

Sub: Closure of S/B A/C

Dear Sir,

    For the last five years, I have been maintaining a Savings Bank Account in your branch. I have been transferred out to Delhi. I, therefore, would like to close my account number…and withdraw the balance amount remaining in my account. Unused cheque leaves are being returned to you.

    Thanking you,

Yours faithfully,
Name

Requesting Bank to Pay Telephone Bills from Account

Address
Dated

The Manager
State Bank of India
Ullasnagar

Sub: Requesting Bank to Pay Telephone Bills from the Account

Dear Sir,

    I have been maintaining a Savings Bank Account No… in your branch. Sometimes I forget to pay my telephone bill in time causing me embarrassment. Therefore, I request you to pay the bills raised against my telephone no…henceforth, from my above said S/B A/C in a timely manner.

Thanking you,

Yours faithfully,
Name

E-mails

E-mails or Electronic mails are written in a manner quite similar to the postal letters. Both have nearly identical composition. In e-mails, name and address of the sender is written on the left and the date on the right side.

The main consideration is that the appearance should be attractive. There are no hard and fast rules. Communicating via e-mails has become very popular and common throughout the world, today. Following are a few examples :

(Sample-1)

Dear Sunil Saxenaji,

I have seen your photograph and gone through the profile. I liked it but still I would be pleased to meet in person. Both of us belong to Delhi. And there is a direct flight connecting New York to Delhi. When do you propose to arrive here? Kindly inform us. In case, the marriage gets solemnised, will I be able to get a visa promptly and move to America with you?

Awaiting your mail!

Yours,
Deepti

The e-mail contains the sender"s e-mail ID. Hence, there is no special need to write separately.

Reply to the Above E-mail

Dear Deepti,

I received your mail. It pleased me no end to know you liked my profile in the first instance itself. I fell for you no sooner I saw your details even though there was no photo of yours. Now I have your picture. I have become an American citizen presently and that there would be no issue getting a visa for you. We can fly to America together. I am sure you would get a good job here.

I am reaching Delhi some time next month. I would inform you the date after getting a confirmed ticket. Please address me by my name. There is no need to write my surname.

Yours,
Sunil

While writing e-mails, it is not necessary to write the subject line. It can be simply done away with. Without so much as a salutation, the person in question can be addressed directly. The sender can, if he so desires, can place his name and address on the right side instead of mentioning on the left side.

(Sample-2)

Vinod Acharya
20, Archana Apartments
Paschim Vihar
New Delhi

Dear Anurag,

I hope you have settled down in Chicago properly. I am quite happy in India. I have consciously decided not to relocate to America since I am under family obligations to take care of.

I hope you will send a reply soon.

Your friend,
Vinod

Confirmatory Copy : Anurag Shukla
                              Crawford Street
                              Chicago (USA)

मॉडर्न लेटर राइटिंग कोर्स

लेखक: अरुण सागर 'आनन्द'

टाइप: पेपरबैक

भाषा: हिन्दी

पृष्ठ: 288 *(with CD)*

मूल्य: ₹ 195

इस पुस्तक में सरल एवं व्यावहारिक हिन्दी मे पत्र व्यवहार के लगभग उन सभी प्रकार के पत्रों को समाहित करने का प्रयास किया गया है जिससे व्यक्ति अपने स्वजनों तथा सामाजिक कार्यों के लिए हिन्दी में पत्र व्यवहार कर सके। प्रस्तुत पुस्तक **'मॉडर्न लेटर राइटिंग कोर्स'** मात्र 30 दिन का कोर्स है। पुस्तक के साथ मुफ्त सीडी ( ) भी दी जा रही है जिसमें हिन्दी में दिये गये पत्रों का अंग्रेजी में अनुवाद भी है। इस पुस्तक में अनौपचारिक पत्र (पारिवारिक पत्र, सगे संबंधी एवं मित्रों को लिखे जाने वाले पत्र) तथा औपचारिक पत्र (सरकारी, गैर-सरकारी तथा अर्ध-सरकारी प्रार्थनापत्र, संपादक को पत्र एवं व्यावसायिक पत्र) समाहित हैं। हिन्दी में पत्र लेखन सिखाने के लिए यह एक अत्यंत उपयोगी पुस्तक है।

हमारी सभी पुस्तकें www.vspublishers.com पर उपलब्ध हैं

पर्सनैलिटी डेवेलपमेंट कोर्स

लेखक: अरुण सागर 'आनन्द'

टाइप: पेपरबैक

भाषा: हिन्दी

पृष्ठ: 304

मूल्य: ₹ 195

किसी भी मनुष्य की सफलता या असफलता में उसके व्यक्तित्व की अहम भूमिका होती है। सभी लोग समाज में सफल होने के लिए अपने व्यक्तित्व को निखारना चाहते हैं। उनका व्यक्तित्व ही उनकी पहचान होती है। अपने व्यक्तित्व के दम पर ही व्यक्ति आम लोगों में कुछ खास नज़र आता है। प्रत्येक व्यक्ति जीवन में कुछ खास करना चाहता है तथा कुछ खास बनना चाहता है। बाजार की जरूरत और आम आदमी की माँग को ध्यान में रखकर यह पुस्तक प्रकाशित की गयी है। बाजार में यह अपने ढंग की अकेली पुस्तक है।

प्रस्तुत पुस्तक मात्र 30 दिन में सम्पूर्ण व्यक्तित्व विकास हेतु सरल एवं आधुनिक कोर्स पर आधारित अवश्य पठनीय पुस्तक है। अनेक चित्रों से सुसज्जित यह पुस्तक आठ भागों में विभाजित की गयी है। प्रत्येक भाग को भी छोटे-छोटे संभागों में बाँटा गया है। सभी संभाग अपने आप में पूर्ण हैं। पुस्तक में उदाहरण व केस स्टडिज़ सहित बात को सरल एवं स्पष्ट शब्दों में समझाया गया है। प्रत्येक दिन के लिए एक अध्याय सामान्य व्यक्ति के सामर्थ्य एवं समय के अनुसार लिखा गया है। यह पुस्तक व्यक्तित्व विकास के गुर से ओतप्रोत है।

हमारी सभी पुस्तकें www.vspublishers.com पर उपलब्ध हैं

www.ingramcontent.com/pod-product-compliance
Lightning Source LLC
Chambersburg PA
CBHW080546230426
43663CB00015B/2732